The Sparkle Effect

10 POWERFUL CONCEPTS TO AWAKEN YOUR BRILLIANCE

Compiled by

SUZANNE CASTLE

with

Jessica Lyonford

Brianna Ruelas

Kreda McCullough

Megan Bozzuto

Micah James

Dr. Christi Monk Andrews

Deborah Jenkins

Dee Armstrong

Trish Reed

Published by Prominence Publishing.

ISBN: 978-1-990830-96-9 (paperback)
        978-1-990830-97-6 (ebook)

Table of Contents

The Sparkle Effect in Action

Most business books are boring. Stiff. Predictable. They either drown you in dry, lifeless tips or hype you up with vague inspiration but leave you with zero clue what to actually do.

I wanted to create something different.

Something that grabs you by the shoulders, gets you fired up, and then hands you a **real, usable** roadmap to take action. Because feeling inspired is nice, but *moving*—actually shifting your life and business forward—is where the magic happens.

That's where *The Sparkle Effect* was born.

This book isn't here to be admired on your shelf. It's not something you read once and forget about. This book is a **tool.** It's meant to be highlighted, underlined, dog-eared. Scribble in the margins. Dream on the pages. Argue with it if you need to. But whatever you do, **use it.**

If you're reading the digital version, don't think you're off the hook—fire up your Notes app, grab a journal, or start a fresh doc and get to work. The format doesn't matter. What matters is that you don't just consume this book—you *interact* with it.

This is a workbook for your momentum. A playbook for your *actual* life.

Because stuck is not a destination. It's a state of mind—and this book is your way out.

THE WOMEN IN THIS BOOK GET IT

Every chapter you're about to read is written by a woman who has been in the trenches of uncertainty. These authors come from different industries, backgrounds, and experiences, but they all have one thing in common: **they decided to move.**

They didn't wait for permission. They didn't sit around hoping for the "perfect time." They made a move, even when it was messy. They built their businesses, took risks, chased their dreams, and figured it out along the way. And now? They're here to share exactly how you can do it, too.

They're not here to impress you. They're here to **equip you.**

Every chapter in this book is a **lesson wrapped in a story.** You're not just getting motivation—you're getting strategy. You'll walk away with bold, practical steps to get unstuck, move past hesitation, and start showing up like the powerhouse you are.

WHAT THIS BOOK WILL DO FOR YOU

The Sparkle Effect isn't about waiting for clarity—it's about creating it. Inside, you'll learn how to:

- Make decisions without overthinking yourself into oblivion

- Lead with impact, without second-guessing every move

- Take bold action before you feel "ready" (spoiler: *no one ever feels ready*)

- Step into possibility and success without waiting for someone to hand it to you

- Build a mindset that keeps you motivated, even when things feel hard

YOUR SPARKLY NEXT STEP

This book is going to push you. It's going to call you out on the places where you've been waiting instead of moving. It's going to make you take a hard look at the ways you've been playing small.

But it's also going to hand you the power to change it.

You don't need another pep talk. You need a plan. And that's exactly what you'll find in these pages.

So don't just read this book—**work the book.** Let these stories challenge you. Let the strategies wake you up. Take the notes. Do the work. Mark up the pages. And if you're reading digitally? **Highlight, type notes, grab a journal—whatever it takes to make this book an active part of your journey.**

Because big dreams don't come to life in the waiting room of *someday.*

They happen when you choose to take the first step—even if it's messy, even if it's small, even if you're still figuring it out as you go.

So go ahead. Get ready to take action.

The life you want isn't waiting. It's yours to claim.

CHAPTER 1

Decision Fatigue is Stealing Your Sparkle—Let's Steal It Back

By Dr. Suzanne Castle

Have you ever been standing in the grocery store, staring at thirty different jars of pasta sauce, and suddenly felt like your entire life is crumbling? No? Just me?

It's 7 PM. You're exhausted. You've answered 153 emails, been on back-to-back calls, and you still have a to-do list that's giving you the side-eye. But somehow, *this*—this moment in the pasta aisle—is where your brain completely shuts down.

Do you get the garlic and herb? The organic basil? Oh wait, this one has truffle oil. Fancy. But hold on, that one's on sale. You blink, and suddenly it's been ten minutes, and you're still standing there like a confused statue in front of a wall of marinara.

That, my friend, is decision fatigue, and it's sneaky.

It doesn't just show up in grocery stores. It shows up in your business when you can't decide if you should launch that offer or wait until the stars magically align. It shows up in life when you spend three hours scrolling through vacation rentals but never actually book the trip.

I know this feeling all too well.

There was a time when every part of my life felt like that pasta aisle—too many choices, not enough energy. On the outside, it looked like I had it all together. Performer. Speaker. The woman who seemed to have her sparkle in check. But behind the scenes? Chaos. My world had fallen apart piece by piece, and I was frozen in place.

Decisions? Please. I was lucky if I could decide whether to get off the bathroom floor.

But here's the truth I learned during that dark season: It's not the big, sweeping decisions that rebuild a life. It's the small, unglamorous ones. The tiny steps you take when everything feels too heavy.

And those small decisions? They're how I stole my sparkle back.

But let's be real—it's not just pasta aisles and rock-bottom moments that send us spiraling into indecision. **I've seen it everywhere. I've lived it everywhere.** Not just in life's biggest, hardest moments, but in the **small, everyday choices** that slowly drain your confidence and momentum. And if there's one truth I've come to believe, it's this:

Waiting for the "perfect" decision is just another way of staying stuck.

I've spent my life balancing two worlds—the creative and the strategic, the artistic and the analytical. I hold degrees in **musical theatre and elementary education**, a **Master of Divinity**, and a **Doctorate in Worship**—because I've always been fascinated by how people think, connect, and grow. I've studied **neuroscience, coaching, goal-setting, and leadership** because I wanted to understand how we move past hesitation and into action.

I've been a performer and an educator, an author and an award-winning speaker, a sought-after keynoter, and a business strategist. My family worked in the oil industry, but I worked the creative world—producing large-scale events, building businesses, and helping leaders step into their power.

And because of all that, I know something really, really well: **decision spirals.**

The ones where you second-guess every move. The ones where you spin in *What-If Land* so long that you talk yourself out of even trying. The ones where the pressure of choosing the *right* thing keeps you from choosing *anything* at all.

I know them because I've lived them.

I also know how to **hack your brain, disrupt the cycle, and start making bold, sustainable moves** that build the life and business you actually want. The kind that get you unstuck, get you moving, and get you results—without the exhaustion.

And that's exactly what we're about to do.

Decision fatigue might be sneaky, but it's not permanent. You can outsmart it. You can hack your brain, disrupt the overwhelm, and start making bold, aligned decisions again.

No more standing frozen in the pasta aisle of your own life.

It's time to move forward—with clarity, confidence, and, yes, a little *sparkle*.

MEET THE SPARKLE-STEALING SQUAD

Let me introduce you to some familiar faces—the undercover agents stealing your sparkle and keeping you stuck. They're subtle, sneaky, and oh-so-relatable. But the good news? Once you recognize them, you can outsmart them.

There's **Overthinking Olivia**, spinning in circles like she's training for the mental Olympics. Olivia loves research. She's got five tabs open, two planners half-filled, and a sticky note mountain that could qualify as modern art. Olivia believes that if she just thinks hard enough, she'll make the *perfect* decision. But we both know that perfect never shows up.

I remember channeling my inner Olivia when I was first thinking about launching a new program. I spent *weeks researching* platforms, comparing tools, and asking for feedback—and got absolutely nowhere. Eventually, I realized no amount of thinking would make the decision for me.

> **Sparkle Strategy:** Put Olivia on a timer for 10 minutes. Make the best decision you can in that window and MOVE ON. Progress beats perfection every time. (Let's be honest, no one's zooming in on that Instagram post anyway.)

Then there's **Cautious Carla**, carefully tiptoeing through life, terrified of making the wrong move. Carla's comfort zone has throw pillows and snacks—it's cozy in there. I used to be Carla when it came to pitching myself for speaking gigs. What if they said no? What if I wasn't good enough? Well, I got tired of waiting for the "perfect time" and started sending the emails anyway.

> **Sparkle Strategy:** Ask yourself, *What will I learn if this doesn't go as planned?* That simple question turns fear into curiosity and makes taking the next step a little less scary.

Ah, **Procrastinating Patty**. She's got plans—big, beautiful, exciting plans—but she'll start them tomorrow. Or next week. Or after she reorganizes her entire workspace. Patty once showed up when I delayed creating content because I didn't have the "right lighting." (Spoiler: I filmed it anyway, and guess what? Nobody cared about the lighting.)

> **Sparkle Strategy:** When Patty shows up, pick ONE tiny task and do it today. One email, one call, one post. Momentum loves movement.

And, of course, there's **Perfect Polly**. Polly is the queen of tweaking. She'll spend days perfecting a landing page, endlessly revising copy, or reworking that one sentence that already sounded great three versions ago. Perfection kept Polly (and me) from launching way too many things on time.

> **Sparkle Strategy:** Commit to 80% done and hit SEND. Seriously. Done is always better than perfect. The world needs your brilliance, not your perfection.

And finally, no messy decision party would be complete without **Info Isabella**. Oh, Isabella loves to learn. She's a regular at the University of Google and has enrolled herself in every free webinar. Isabella makes you *feel* productive because research *looks* like work. But all that learning without action? It's a shiny distraction. I've been Isabella, stuck in analysis, convincing myself I'd move forward after "just one more article."

> **Sparkle Strategy:** Set a 20-minute research limit. Then, decide and ACT. Google won't make the decision for you, but it will gladly keep you stuck.

Recognizing these sparkle-stealers is only half the battle. The real magic? Taking back control, one small, intentional step at a time.

WHY TINY STEPS CREATE MASSIVE SPARKLE

Let's circle back to that pasta sauce moment. When I was standing in the grocery store, frozen by thirty different jars of marinara, I wasn't just overwhelmed by sauce—I was overwhelmed by *choice*. And that's how decision fatigue sneaks in.

Here's what I learned: The way out of that mental gridlock isn't making a massive, life-changing decision. It's picking a jar of sauce. Any jar. Just make the smallest move forward.

That's exactly how I started rebuilding my life when it felt like everything was crumbling. I wasn't in a place to make big, bold decisions. I had to start small. Tiny decisions—like getting out of bed, responding to one email, or eating something other than ice cream—were my version of picking the sauce. Those micro-decisions rewired my brain for momentum. Here's where the science kicks in—and it's pretty sparkly.

Every time you make a small decision and follow through, your brain rewards you with a burst of dopamine. Dopamine is the feel-good chemical that makes you want to keep going. It's like your brain giving you a high-five, saying, "Yes! You did the thing!" That rush of dopamine makes it easier to make the next decision. And then the next. That's how momentum builds—one tiny, unglamorous decision at a time.

But it's not just about feeling good in the moment. This is how new habits form. Small, consistent actions create new neural pathways in your brain. It's called **neuroplasticity**—your brain's ability to adapt and change. Every small step you take strengthens those pathways, making it easier and more natural to take the next one.

Over time, these tiny decisions build momentum. One step leads to another, and suddenly, you're not stuck anymore. You're moving forward with clarity and confidence. And here's the truth: You don't need clarity to make a decision. You need a decision to gain clarity.

Let's bust open one of the biggest lies we've been told: *You need to wait for clarity before making a decision.*

Wrong.

Clarity doesn't show up on its own. It doesn't magically appear after another hour of thinking or another day of waiting. Clarity is a result of taking action—*not* the starting point. The more you wait, the heavier the decision feels. The more you move, the clearer the path becomes.

Think about it. When have you ever gained clarity by sitting still? Waiting feels safe, but it doesn't move you forward. Action—even messy, imperfect action—creates momentum. It reveals what works, what doesn't, and what the next step should be.

Stop waiting. Start moving.

Take Overthinking Olivia, for example. She'll have you researching pasta sauce brands for hours. But if you tell her to grab the garlic and herb and move on, suddenly dinner gets made. That's how micro-decisions work. They bypass the overwhelm and get you moving.

So, if you're stuck in indecision—whether it's launching a new program, hiring help, or just choosing what to post on social media—stop thinking you need to have it all figured out. Start with the smallest action. Send the email. Make the call. Pick the sauce. Because those small steps? They're the quiet heroes behind every bold move. And once you start stacking them, your sparkle comes back stronger than ever.

SPARKLE CHECK-IN: REFLECTION & ACTION

Now that you know who's been stealing your sparkle, it's time to do something about it. Let's pause and reflect—because awareness is the first step to change.

Reflection Prompts

✦ Which Sparkle-Stealer shows up most for me? (Overthinking Olivia, Cautious Carla, Procrastinating Patty, Perfect Polly, or Info Isabella?)

✦ What's one decision I've been avoiding? (Why am I avoiding it, and which Sparkle-Stealer is feeding that hesitation?)

✦ What small action can I take today to move past it? *(It doesn't need to be big—just intentional.)*

✦ How will I celebrate that small win? (Celebrate every single step forward—you deserve it!)

YOUR SPARKLE PEP TALK

Let me be crystal clear: Decision fatigue isn't here to stay, but your sparkle? Oh, honey, that's permanent. It's just been hiding under a pile of overthinking, procrastination, and perfectionism. It's time to clear that clutter and let your brilliance shine through.

You don't need to overhaul your entire life today. You don't need a 10-step action plan or a perfectly color-coded strategy. What you *do* need is to make one small, bold move. That's it.

One step. One decision. Because small steps—like picking a jar of pasta sauce—are what lead to big, bold momentum.

Remember those sneaky sparkle-stealers? Overthinking Olivia, Cautious Carla, Procrastinating Patty, Perfect Polly, and Info Isabella? They might show up again, but now you know how to handle them. You have the tools,   you have the awareness, and most importantly, you have the power to decide that they no longer get to run the show.

Every big success story you admire started with one tiny, brave choice. Someone sent the email, launched the messy version of their offer, or made the imperfect decision and moved forward anyway. That can be you. It *will* be you.

I didn't rebuild my life with grand, sweeping gestures. I rebuilt it by choosing my next step—no matter how small—and moving forward. Now I stand on stages, coach women, and run a business that lights me up. Not because I made one massive decision but because I picked my own damn jar of pasta sauce.

So here's your invitation—no, your challenge: Stop letting indecision dull your shine. Own your power. Make that move. The next step—no matter how small—is where your momentum begins because bold moves aren't made by waiting for the perfect moment. They're made by women who decide to sparkle *right now*.

I want you to imagine this: The confetti is falling, the lights are up, and the spotlight is on YOU. Not next year. Not when everything is perfect. *Now*.

This is your moment.

That email you've been too scared to send? Hit send. That messy offer you've been overthinking? Launch it. That dream you've been whispering to yourself at 2 AM? Say it out loud— and then take a step toward it.

You are not here to blend in. You are here to shine, to lead, and to take up space. The world is waiting for what only *you* can bring—and it's about time you delivered it with fireworks and glitter.

Queens don't stand frozen in grocery aisles forever.

They pick the sauce, toss on their crown, and run the damn world. So go steal your sparkle back—and make the world wonder how they ever lived without it. I'll be here, front row, tossing confetti and cheering you on. Now, go make your next bold move—and maybe dinner while you're at it.

THE SPARKLE EFFECT MANIFESTO

Unleash your power. Own your brilliance. Sparkle without limits.

1. **I AM DONE SHRINKING.** I refuse to dim my light to make others comfortable. I will take up space, speak louder, and show up unapologetically.

2. **I DECIDE.** I make the rules, the moves, and the magic. I own every choice, and I trust myself to figure it out.

3. **ACTION OVER PERFECTION.** I will not wait for perfect conditions. I move boldly and make magic in the messy middle.

4. **FEAR DOESN'T GET A VOTE.** Fear can ride in the car, but it's never getting the keys. I lead with courage, not comfort.

5. **DONE IS BETTER THAN PERFECT.** I will hit send, launch the offer, and make the call. My brilliance doesn't need polishing.

6. **I CREATE MOMENTUM.** One bold move at a time. Small steps lead to big shifts.

7. **MY SPARKLE IS MY POWER.** I will not apologize for who I am. My sparkle is my strategy.

8. **I AM A FORCE.** I rise, I roar, and I reign. I am the CEO of my life.

9. **I MAKE WAVES.** I don't wait for permission. I disrupt, lead, and leave my mark.

10. **I WILL NOT WAIT.** The perfect moment doesn't exist. I will move *now*.

This is my world. My rules. My revolution.

I am not here to play small. I am here to SPARKLE. And nothing will stop me.

Don't stop here. Your sparkle deserves to keep growing and glowing! Head over to suzannecastle.com for free resources, empowering trainings, and tools designed to help you keep that momentum alive. Let's keep building your bold, unstoppable life—one sparkly step at a time.

ABOUT THE AUTHOR

Suzanne Castle is an award-winning business coach, keynote speaker, and founder of The Sparkle Factor®, a revolutionary approach to helping ambitious women break free from overwhelm and achieve bold success. With a career spanning from the stage as a professional entertainer to the boardroom as a strategist and leadership advisor, Suzanne has dedicated her life to empowering women to embrace their unique brilliance.

Recognized with a Bronze Stevie® Award for Women's Business Coach of the Year in 2024, Suzanne has been named one of the top 10 most inspirational and engaging women in Tarrant County. Her expertise and captivating style have landed her features on every major television network. Known for blending neuroscience-backed strategies with creativity, Suzanne's work is grounded in helping women take decisive action to design the life and business of their dreams.

Beyond her professional accomplishments, Suzanne is celebrated for her relatable humor, sparkly energy, and passion for helping others thrive. Whether speaking on international stages, coaching one-on-one, or leading transformative workshops, Suzanne inspires others to move boldly forward with clarity and confidence. She believes firmly that "stuck is never the furthest you can go."

Check out suzannecastle.com for a special goodie download!

CHAPTER 2

How to Live and Lead With Happiness

By Jessica Lyonford

If you'd met me in high school, you'd never have pegged me as a future happiness expert. Quite the opposite, in fact. My teenage years were marked by insecurity, overachievement, and a gnawing sense that I wasn't enough—no matter how much I excelled on paper. My twenties didn't improve things much. I had the big job, the big paycheck, and the big burnout to match. I was living the kind of life that looked perfect from the outside, but on the inside, I was barely holding it together.

Would I go back and rewrite that chapter of my life? Absolutely not. That chapter, however messy, shaped me into who I am today. She—the insecure teenager, the exhausted young professional—led me here. Whether she realized it or not, her struggles became my lessons, and those lessons became my purpose.

Today, I'm a happiness consultant, teaching people how to live and lead with happiness. This work isn't about helping people feel good (though that's part of it). It's about building a new kind of leadership—a kind I call *Happy Leadership*.

Happy Leaders show up with confidence, authenticity, and compassion. They lead thriving teams, nurture households with optimism, and inspire communities to aim higher and care deeper. They're proof that happiness and success aren't opposing forces but powerful partners.

And here's the best part:

There's a Happy Leader inside you.

And I'm here to show you how to bring them to life.

OWN YOUR STORY

To live and lead with happiness, you first have to own your story—all of it. That means making peace with the messy, painful, or unfinished parts.

For me, owning my story meant confronting my burnout and depression head-on. I had to stop pretending everything was fine and ask the hard questions: Why wasn't the big paycheck enough? Why didn't the title make me happy? Why was I constantly running on empty?

The answers weren't pretty. I'd spent years chasing success to prove I was worthy. My achievements had become a shield against vulnerability, but that shield came at a cost. I felt disconnected from myself and others.

Owning my story wasn't about blaming myself or anyone else. It was about taking responsibility for how I wanted to move forward. And here's the thing: The same is true for you.

Your story—however complicated—contains your greatest wisdom. The moment you stop running from it is the moment you start owning your power.

> **Reflect on this:** What is one challenge from your past that has shaped who you are today? How has it influenced your leadership style?

LET LOVE BE YOUR GUIDE

Leadership and happiness have something in common: both thrive when fueled by love.

Now, when I say love, I'm not just talking about romantic relationships. I mean the kind of love that lights you up—whether it's love for people, passions, or problems you feel called to solve.

For me, this meant reconnecting with the things that gave my life meaning. I leaned into my passion for helping others and my fascination with what makes people thrive. Slowly but surely, I began building a life rooted in what I loved.

Take, for example, a parent who prioritizes connection over perfection. Or a community leader driven by love for their neighborhood. When love fuels your actions, it becomes a powerful compass for where to invest your time and energy.

Reflect on this: What lights you up? Who or what inspires you to show up as your best self? How can you lean into those loves more intentionally today?

HAPPINESS IS A SKILL—PRACTICE IT

I'm going to let you in on a little secret: Happiness isn't a feeling that comes and goes, dependent on luck or circumstances. It's a skill—something you can cultivate and strengthen—like learning to play an instrument or mastering a sport.

At the core of this practice is a framework I call *The Eight Pillars of Happiness*:

1. Confidence
2. Authenticity
3. Compassion
4. Purpose
5. Optimism
6. Curiosity

7. Feeling
8. Gratitude

These are research-backed skill sets that lead to greater well-being, resilience, and joy. There's no hierarchy here—each pillar is equally essential, and they all work together to create a balanced foundation for happiness. Some of these skills might come naturally to you. If so, celebrate that! Others may need a little more intention and effort. Be accountable for that.

Here's how these pillars show up in real life—and how you can start practicing them.

Confidence is about trusting in your worth and abilities. It's not about having all the answers or being the best, but about knowing you can handle the task in front of you. Confidence lets you take risks and pursue your goals, even when you feel uncertain.

Practice it: Reflect on past successes. What strengths helped you achieve them? Use those strengths as anchors when tackling new challenges.

◆◆——————◆——————◆◆

Authenticity is the courage to show up as your true self. It means letting go of perfectionism and aligning how you present yourself with who you really are. When you lead authentically, people trust you more because they can feel your honesty.

Practice it: Start small. Share something vulnerable in a conversation—a challenge you're facing or a lesson you've learned. Notice how it deepens connection.

◆◆————◆————◆◆

Compassion is kindness in action directed toward yourself and others. It's about understanding struggles without judgment and choosing to respond with care. Compassion strengthens relationships and creates a culture of trust and support.

Practice it: When someone makes a mistake—yourself included—pause and ask, *How can I respond with kindness instead of criticism?*

◆◆————◆————◆◆

Purpose is about aligning your actions with what matters most to you. It's the 'why' behind what you do, and it gives even hard work a sense of meaning. Purpose drives fulfillment and resilience.

Practice it: Write down three things that matter most to you—your core values. How can you align your daily choices with those values?

Optimism is the ability to see possibilities, even in challenges. It's not about ignoring problems but about believing in solutions and brighter days ahead. Optimism boosts resilience and helps you navigate setbacks with hope.

Practice it: The next time you're faced with a challenge, ask yourself, *What's one opportunity or lesson this situation offers me?*

Curiosity keeps you open to learning and growing. It's the mindset that helps you see obstacles as puzzles to solve rather than threats to avoid. Curiosity sparks creativity and innovation.

Practice it: Approach a routine task in a new way or ask someone, *What's one thing I wouldn't guess about you?* and see where the conversation leads.

Feeling is about embracing your full emotional range because happiness isn't about forcing positivity—it's about being present with all your emotions, even the hard ones. When you allow yourself to truly feel, you process emotions more effectively and can show up as your true self.

Practice it: When a strong emotion arises, name it. Say, *I feel [emotion]*. This simple act helps you understand and process your feelings rather than suppress them.

Gratitude is the practice of recognizing and appreciating the good in your life. It's about shifting your focus from scarcity to abundance. Gratitude doesn't erase challenges, but it helps you find joy even in difficult times.

Practice it: At the end of each day, write down three things you're grateful for—even if they're small, like a kind word or a good meal.

When you intentionally practice these skills, they become part of your default mindset. Research shows this kind of intentionality works. Studies on gratitude have found that practicing it daily increases happiness and reduces depressive symptoms. Similarly, optimism has been linked to stronger resilience and problem-solving abilities.

The more you practice, the easier these skills become, and as you grow them, you're both improving your own happiness **and** creating a ripple effect that positively impacts everyone around you.

> **Reflect on this:** Which of the Eight Pillars feels most natural to you? Which one could you strengthen? Write down one action you'll take to start building that skill today.

CELEBRATE THE GOOD

In a world full of noise and negativity, it's easy to overlook the good. But here's the thing: what you focus on grows. If you want to live and lead with happiness, you have to intentionally celebrate what's good.

This doesn't mean ignoring life's challenges. In fact, it's the opposite. It means acknowledging the hard stuff while also making space for gratitude and joy. It's about finding balance.

For instance, a leader might start meetings by sharing a recent success story from their team. A parent might end the day by asking their kids to share one thing they're grateful for. Simple practices like these shift focus to the positive and create a culture of appreciation, whether at work or at home.

Research backs this up. Regularly reflecting on three good things each day can improve happiness and reduce depressive symptoms in as little as six weeks.

> **Reflect on this:** What's good in your life right now? What's one way you can celebrate it—personally or with others?

SHARE YOUR LIGHT

Happiness isn't a solo sport.
It's communal.

As humans, we're wired for connection. We need each other to thrive. And the world needs you—your kindness, your insight, and your unique light.

One of the most powerful ways to live and lead with happiness is to share that light with others. Think of the neighbor who organizes a block party to bring people together or the friend who volunteers their time at a local food bank. These acts don't require grand gestures—they're about showing up with intention and choosing to lead with authenticity, compassion, and optimism.

When you do this, you create a ripple effect. Your happiness inspires others to be happier. Your light reminds others to shine theirs.

Reflect on this: How can you share your light today? Maybe it's a small act of kindness, a word of encouragement, or simply being fully present with someone who needs it. Whatever it is, trust that it matters.

BE A HAPPY LEADER

Here's the truth: You're already a leader. Whether you're leading a team, a family, or simply your own life, your choices set the tone for everyone around you. Leadership isn't defined by a title or a job description—it's defined by how you show up in the world.

And every day, you have the opportunity to choose what kind of leader you'll be. Will you lead with stress and reactivity, letting circumstances dictate your mindset? Or will you lead with intention, crafting a life rooted in joy, resilience, and connection?

Being a Happy Leader doesn't mean you're always cheerful or free from challenges. It means you're committed to the practices that build happiness, both for yourself and for others. It means showing up with Confidence, staying Authentic, extending Compassion, and aligning with your Purpose. It means choosing Optimism when the road is rocky, approaching life with Curiosity, allowing yourself to truly feel your Feelings (yes, all of them!), and celebrating the good things already present with Gratitude.

Happiness is a skill, but it's also a gift—a gift you give to yourself and a gift that radiates out to those around you. Research shows that happiness is contagious. When you cultivate it in yourself, you naturally inspire it in others. This is the ripple effect of happiness, and as a leader, you are uniquely positioned to amplify it.

Imagine a world where more people embraced this kind of leadership. Where workplaces were built on Curiosity and Optimism, households were guided by Compassion and Gratitude, and communities were strengthened by Purpose and Authenticity. That world starts with one decision: your decision to lead with happiness.

So, take a moment to reflect. What kind of leader do you want to be? What legacy do you want to leave—not just in your career, but in the lives you touch every day? The Happy Leader inside you is ready to shine. The only thing left to do is give them permission.

Take that first step. Start small if you need to—celebrate one good thing, extend one act of kindness, or take one courageous step toward your purpose. It all adds up. It all matters. And so do you.

The world doesn't just need leaders. It needs *Happy Leaders*. And I know you're ready to be one.

ABOUT THE AUTHOR

Jessica Lyonford is a designer of happiness and best-selling author of *The Happy Leader Playbook: A Science-Backed Guide to Supercharging Energy and Impact.* As a speaker, consultant and coach, she blends real-world experience, science and actionable insights to transform workplace culture. Her keynotes and workshops show leaders and teams how the science of happiness and human flourishing can supercharge collaboration, creativity and results.

Jessica works with leaders to design processes, environments and systems that empower growth and well-being—at work, at home and in the community. Her holistic approach proves that happiness isn't just personal—it's the key to thriving organizations.

With her engaging style and deep expertise, Jessica inspires audiences to see happiness as their ultimate leadership advantage. She's committed to creating spaces where people feel seen, valued, and inspired to show up as their best selves. Because when people flourish, businesses thrive.

Visit www.jessicalyonford.com for tools and resources to design a life—and leadership—for happiness.

CHAPTER 3

Choosing Possibility Over Limitation

By Brianna Ruelas

Have you ever been caught sleepwalking? I remember a conversation I had with my husband about a premise known as the "ten-year nap." Oddly enough, this "nap" occurs when we are fully awake and suggests that the perpetual chaos and distractions we prioritize in life cause us to sleepwalk, wasting years of our lifetime in the interim. Fast forward five or even ten years later, and we find ourselves stuck doing the same old thing, in a pattern of apathy and boredom because we obliviously choose a lackluster life. But is that what we *really* want? A lackluster life void of color, adventure, passion, and joy?

Early in my singing career, I had big dreams, but no clue on how to reach them. I found myself wandering, "Lost in La La Land," but when an opportunity arrived to try out for a new show called, "American Idol," it reignited a fire inside. I was rejected three times before getting my golden ticket yes, and moving on to become a Top 100 Finalist out of 100,000 who auditioned for Season 4. The grit developed with every no, pushed me to persevere, and energized me with the tangible awareness that I was indeed, "alive!" Although the curtains closed on that experience much sooner than I would've liked, it served as a beginning, *not* an end, and would lead to many more adventures in life, including becoming a multi-best-selling author, keynote speaker, podcast host, and the Founder of the motivational, creative strategy company, The Ruelas Music Group. But all of this couldn't happen if I was sleepwalking.

The problem with sleepwalking is that it keeps us stuck in a complacency cycle, giving fear full rein to permeate and dominate our days. This complacency cycle leads us to believe that safety and protocol are best as we develop faulty thinking and coach ourselves to not rock the boat or make waves. We believe we must "take one for the team," regardless of whether it diminishes our light or minimizes the great contribution we were born to make. Within this complacency cycle, we come to expect a linear path, but when the path becomes a winding road stacked with boulders, hills, and unforeseen events, we cower in fear. We also become paralyzed by the idea of trying something new or the mere notion of stepping out in faith. Although we inherently know that different actions lead to different results, we settle for being stuck and stagnant and avoid the unknown that newness brings. Over time, we care for ourselves less and less and inadvertently make way for procrastination, anxiety, and burnout. A toxic web has spun, silencing our confidence and trapping our ability to create and innovate.

When you normalize this way of living and lose your confidence, brain fog and low-grade depression become commonplace. Friends and family who know you best may say, "I'm worried about you. I haven't seen that spark or twinkle in your eye in a long time." When you look at yourself in the mirror, you see sadness, defeat, and exhaustion. Your smile has changed over the years, as you've allowed circumstances to impact your self-confidence, and you no longer prioritize how to show up for yourself daily. Your zest for life somehow got swallowed up in the dark abyss of "meh," leaving only remnants of motivation and possibility in its wake. You've become a walking, breathing, limitation factory *but* if you're brave enough to acknowledge it, you may also uncover that still voice inside, reminding you, "It's never too late to wake up and start again."

I know what it feels like to live in self-imposed limitation and succumb to the drag of life, being dragged along to where years of chronic stress, fear, and loss can often lead. I've experienced varied highs and lows, and, despite my array of accomplishments, I've been sucked into believing the lie that I was a failure. I've struggled to celebrate the great work I did and the milestones I reached. I've also been a slave to a destructive mindset, only focusing on all that is wrong versus all that is going right. I've wrestled with doubt and battled the negative self-talk swirling in my mind, ignoring the truth that I was indeed a success. Despite my accomplishments, I struggled to appreciate and celebrate how far I'd come. I was always looking around the corner to see what was next. I stacked my calendar with obligations and struggled to enjoy the gifts of the present.

When the challenges of entrepreneurship took a toll on my psyche and led to financial insecurity for our family, I befriended shame and doubted my gifts mattered. *Who was I to believe that I could actually make a difference? What a joke.* I fed the chatter in my mind with more garbage and couldn't see what others saw in me—that I was indeed a bright light. It took slowing down, sitting with my grief, and some massive encouragement from other successful women to remind me that I was a success in the making. The same goes for *you.*

You, too, are a future success story.

In fact, you are a success-making machine, but like me, you must believe that to be true and take the first step.

Ultimately, your faith and belief in yourself have to be louder than the naysayers and your negative self-talk. Your faith and belief have to be greater than the fear, rejection, and failures that challenge you to stand down and give up. You must unapologetically and intentionally pursue the *one* thing you believe you are being called and led to and trust that all steps will be revealed **as you step.** You must believe that your collective experiences, good and bad, all matter because they've shaped you into the powerful force you are today. As you lean into the discomfort, embracing that your path will not always be linear, you can trust with expectancy that you are being divinely protected and guided.

When we full-heartedly believe that our gifts, light, and message matter, we position ourselves to realize some of our greatest, most profound, and most meaningful contributions to this world. Harnessing courage is key as we take the first step, and with each subsequent step, new possibilities and renewed confidence are revealed. Rejecting a cycle of complacency, however uncomfortable it may feel, expands our belief system and roots us in purpose and faith.

So, what does it look like to choose possibility over limitation, and how can we get started? Over the years, I've noted what helped me bounce back from self-doubt and decision fatigue and increased my confidence and belief. Inside this chapter, I'll be sharing three tangible steps you can implement in your life, and it all begins with how you start your morning.

STEP ONE | DEVELOP YOUR DAILY PRACTICE

Whether you're an early riser or a late one, how you start your day matters. A routine that includes physical, mental, and spiritual practices can make a huge difference in your mindset, motivation, and focus. When I find myself trudging through life, I almost always trace back those funky feelings to an interruption in my personal habits for daily success. With a majority of working women feeling chronic stress in their day-to-day lives, maintaining a calm demeanor can feel daunting and out of reach. Chronic stress can also lead to overwhelm, so protecting our peace while combating anxiety should be a top priority. Creating a set of daily practices for our lives that become "non-negotiables" enables us to tap into an endless well of strength and encouragement. Getting started is half the battle, but when we commit to putting one foot in front of the other and showing up for ourselves even when we feel like giving up, momentum will grow and drive our progress.

THE FIERCE FIVE: 5 MORNING SUCCESS HABITS FOR A DAILY SPIRITUAL PRACTICE

HABIT ONE: EXERCISE

Whether it's a walk or run outside or hitting the Pilates studio, a little fresh air and oxygen to the brain does a body wonders! It's also scientifically proven to increase focus because increased blood flow gives our brain nutrients. Some of my freshest revelations and creative ideas have come through stepping away from my screen and getting active because movement inspires momentum.

HABIT TWO: BE STILL

It might feel counterintuitive to go from activating through exercise to being still, but stillness is a very important step toward focus and productivity. How can we expect to receive guidance and wisdom when we are running around like a chicken with their head cut off all the time? Distractions and over-committed calendars create clutter. Prioritizing time to quiet the mind and clear the cobwebs, even if it's just five minutes in the morning, provides a special grounding for our day. This can be in the form of a quick meditation or prayer, but the key is to open ourselves up to listen and not ask. Stillness can bring on discomfort, but the rewards of sticking with it are great, including increased mental and spiritual well-being and improved stress management.

HABIT THREE: RECEIVE SOME INSPIRATION AND TRUTH!

The information we receive at the top of our day matters, so consuming something inspirational, either from a motivational podcast, music playlist, or faith-based book, can position us with confidence and motivation as we approach each day.

HABIT FOUR: REFLECT AND JOURNAL

After taking time to be still and receive some truth, take a moment to reflect. Where have your thoughts been focused, and do they need redirection? If you received a nudge or word from that still voice, write it down and consider how you might take action on it.

HABIT FIVE: PRACTICE GRATITUDE

Give Thanks! Be thankful for all the goodness of the seen, unseen, and yet to come. Enter your day with an expectant heart. Anticipate the beauty to come.

When we are out of our rhythm, feeling stuck, down, or anxious, we limit our impact on the world and cut ourselves off from feeling peace. The good news is that a strong daily practice can become a healthy habit that fuels you with determination, confidence, and peace.

STEP TWO | TAKE OUT THE TRASH

To step into limitless possibility and offer our best to the world around us, we must let go of the mental clutter that we cling to, including the harmful thoughts, habits, and tendencies that hinder our progress. Throughout my life, I've experienced seasons where my life became one big comparison party. In college, I lacked what all the other wealthy, pretty girls on campus had. When I was pursuing music, I felt late to the game and didn't have that "edge" all the younger artists had. In my green entrepreneurial years, I scrolled endlessly on social media at what everyone else was doing and thought their massive email lists and picture-perfect branding meant I was doing something wrong. This obsession with everyone else hijacked my joy and wasted too much time. I sought to replicate their model instead of tapping into the uniqueness that I brought to the table.

Thankfully, time is a teacher, and I learned that mental clutter, in the form of distractions, fear, and self-doubt, blocks us from stepping into the magnificence we were designed for. Striving and comparing sets the tone for false confidence based on the standards of others instead of our internal compass. Cultivating our own fertile soil positions us to make an impact.

One way to ensure we're preparing to bloom is to take inventory. A personal inventory will help you identify any mental clutter that needs to be removed so you can uncover a significant piece of the puzzle of life: belief in yourself. Below are 5 Personal Inventory Questions you can write down and answer in your journal to get started:

---

5 Personal Inventory Questions

1. HOW am I speaking to myself these days? (With Compassion? Critique? Sarcasm?)

2. WHERE am I thriving, and WHERE am I drowning?

3. WHAT do I *really* want for myself?

4. WHAT junk, negativity, or trash do I need to take out?

5. WHAT is one piece of action I want to take? WHAT is my first step?

STEP THREE | SERVE FROM THE SAUCER

Would you agree that the majority of people are bombarded by advice daily? Whether it's through a well-meaning friend or family member, a social media post, or even this amazing book, it can sometimes present as an unwelcome intrusion. However, wise counsel can sometimes hit us differently, catching us at the right place and time to thoughtfully receive it.

The month before I celebrated my fortieth trip around the sun, I won a trip for two to Napa. I didn't even remember entering this contest, so when I received the congratulatory email, I thought it was spam! It was the perfect mini-vacation for my husband and me, and while there, I had a very meaningful encounter with a shaman. She asked for permission to tell me something personal about *me*. She saw something in the lines of my hands and felt compelled to share her message: "Brianna, you are a light, and you must shine. Those who come into your light need you and are there for a reason, **but your cup must runneth over, and you must serve from the saucer.**" Now mind you, this shaman and I had connected just briefly in that short weekend, but her advice was extremely profound because I had never even considered the *saucer*! My focus has always been on the *cup*.

The issue with focusing *only* on "filling our cup" is that we need all those energetic contents to sustain our own well-being. And with a substantial part of our joy coming from contribution, we will eventually have to dip into the contents of that cup to serve others around us. That leads to draining our cup and potential burnout. So yes, we must fill our cup, but we must also allow it to *overflow* in order to share our gifts with others. Ultimately, we can't make a memorable impact in the hearts of those at work, our community, or our family and friends when we're depleted or wrapped up in the noise and busyness of our lives.

Neglecting our mental well-being and becoming spread thin by being "busy" makes us prone to anxiety and leads to misalignment with the place and space in which we are called. We lose our sense of peace as we waste time, resources, and our ability to make an impact! When we're so busy being "busy," we cannot show up as the best of ourselves or create at the level required for innovation. With over-commitment, we also deprioritize our personal habits for daily success and ignore that little tap on the shoulder, guiding us to what is NEXT.

You have a very significant and unique contribution to make in this world, but sometimes we get so busy that we miss the clues. Are you missing the clues? What are you blocking yourself from stepping into because you're too busy to hear or see what's next for you? If you're thinking, "I'm behind" or "It's too late for me," I'm here to tell you, *you're right on time.* By the simple act of showing up for yourself and taking the time to read this book, you show your commitment to growth and curiosity. You surely care about making your mark amongst your friends, family, and community. But this is not about doing more. It's about saying no to the distractions that knock you out of alignment and being intentional with how you choose to use your time and energy.

◆◆——————◆——————◆◆

LIVE LIMITLESS

It's time to consider whether you're feeling pulled to show up differently in the world around you and what your first step might look like. What whisper have you been ignoring? The desire was placed on your heart for a reason, and it's time to get clear on your contribution, embrace possibility, and live limitless! As a keynote speaker and singer, I spend time writing original music that I incorporate into my talks. The lyrics are intentional and always reinforce the message, providing encouragement and motivation. This song is my reminder to you that you are limitless. I invite you to check out the lyrics and enjoy the studio recording through the QR code below:

Limitless, By Brianna Ruelas & Jo James
Production By Adam Pickrell

Are you waiting for permission?
For someone to tell you, "Let Go"
Living in the past keeps you hidden.
There's beauty unfolding, up the road
It's all in the Overflow.
Get Ready For A New Season
Soak in the Brilliance of Who You Are
It's up to you
It's time to claim it
What you seek is not too far
It's All In The Overflow
Boldly Freely
Step Into Your Light
Forward, Fearless, Heading to New Heights
Say Yes, Say Yes, Say Yes
Believe, You Are Limitless
Just Say Yes.

For more encouragement or to book a keynote concert, connect with Brianna at briannaruelasmusic.com and stream *Limitless* on Spotify through the QR code:

ABOUT THE AUTHOR

Brianna Ruelas is a Keynote Speaker/ Singer, Creative Strategist, Multi-Book Author, and Podcaster, who takes her collective gifts, experience, and passion wherever she goes. In her Keynotes, Brianna integrates LIVE performance & original music with teaching, to reinforce key concepts that ignite Motivation, Innovation, and Action. As a mother to three girls, Brianna has a heart for our future female leaders, inspiring her to launch the podcast, Campus Bread, to help college women feel "less alone" and more connected as they grow in faith and friendship. From gracing the stage of American Idol Season 4, to Corporate Sales at Disney, supporting her Restaurateur husband, and acting as the Founder of Ruelas Music Group, Brianna is passionate about positioning others to thrive, while creating meaningful impact in the world. For more encouragement and motivation, follow her on Instagram @briannaruelasmusic.

CHAPTER 4

Where Are My Leads?

By Kreda McCullough

Today, I stand as a messaging alignment strategist who's guided over 300 businesses to refine their branding and connect with right-fit clients, through many facets of marketing—graphic design, brand strategy, messaging, content, and copywriting.

All so they can attract quality leads.

I've trained and coached leaders inside organizations like Rocky Mountain MicroFinance Institute, the Black Business Initiative, and Denver Metro SBDC, helping women solo-preneurs, firm owners, and executive coaches break free from cookie-cutter corporate talk and AI-generated content buzzwords. I help them confidently position themselves, refine their messaging, and stand out in a saturated marketplace—without sounding like everyone else using AI.

But I wasn't always seen as the expert I am today.

For years, I was stuck in a cycle of being underpaid and underestimated, not because I lacked the skills, but because I was playing small.

I'll never forget the days when clients treated me like I was just "the designer."

I built my first business as a graphic designer, believing my work alone would make people see my value. I thought that if my designs were good enough, bold enough, and creative enough, clients would naturally recognize me as an authority.

They didn't.

Instead of seeing me as a strategic partner, business owners saw me as a doer, not a thinker. They came to me for flyers and social media graphics, but when I tried to offer deeper positioning insights, they dismissed it.

"Just make it look good."

"We don't need all that strategy, just design something real quick."

"Can you do this flyer for $50?

Fifty. Dollar. Flyer.

Meanwhile, I watched other designers land bigger contracts. They weren't necessarily more talented than me, but they showed up as strategists, not just creatives.

I was working too hard for too little.

And that's when it hit me.

Yes, I am an amazing designer. It's a gift from God, but my calling was deeper.

I wasn't just here to create something that looked good—I was here to lead, to guide, and to elevate businesses through clarity and positioning.

I was built for more.

Then the pandemic hit in 2020.

Design contracts were gone.

The small businesses, churches, and organizations I worked with either cut their marketing budgets or shut down completely. My graphic design business was hanging on by a thread and I was chasing design jobs that didn't pay what I deserved.

Then, divine intervention showed up in my inbox.

Scrolling through emails one day, I saw what looked like a message from an organization I belonged to. It was advertising a free masterclass for women entrepreneurs who wanted to make $50K a year.

I was barely making four figures, so you better believe I signed up!

Stepping into that virtual room, I saw one familiar face and thought, "Well damn, everybody else in this organization must be making $50K or more."

I almost let imposter syndrome take me out right there.

But God had bigger plans.

That masterclass changed everything.

I walked in thinking, *Maybe I'll learn a few business tips.* I walked out realizing, I've been playing small, and it's costing me.

I invested in the program, found a coach who actually saw me and showed me that success wasn't about changing who I was, it was about stepping fully into who God called me to be.

That realization sparked something bigger than I expected.

I wasn't just creating pretty graphics anymore, or begging people to see my value. I was helping businesses tell their authentic stories through visuals and strategy.

THE SHIFT THAT CHANGED MY BUSINESS

After my own rebrand in 2020, my revenue jumped from four figures to multiple five figures. I transitioned from just designing brands to strategically building them.

I became a Certified Brand Strategist and started working with businesses to refine their positioning, helping them stand out in their market. I helped them create messaging that made people pay attention and developed content strategies that attracted quality leads.

For the first time, I was working with clients who valued my expertise.

But it gets better…

In 2022, I stumbled across AI tools, and at first, I wasn't even thinking about how they could impact my business. I was using them as research tools. But the more I explored, the more I realized these weren't just tools for tech nerds. Used correctly, they could help businesses refine their messaging, create content faster, and identify what actually resonated with their audience.

I was hooked.

I became so passionate about the power of AI tools that I went all in, earning my certification as an AI Consultant to help businesses integrate AI ethically and strategically.

AI tools gave me real-time insights into what words and phrases connected with my audience. It was like having a personal assistant that I could train to use my brand voice and help me create content more efficiently.

But as excited as I was, I quickly found out that most business owners weren't.

They were afraid.

Some thought AI was going to replace them. Some thought it would strip the personality out of their writing. Others were so overwhelmed with all the talk about it, they avoided it altogether.

But here's what they didn't see...

While they were hesitating, opportunities were passing them by.

If you're a business owner, sitting on the sidelines, worried about robots taking over, your competitors are already using AI tools to analyze customer behavior and write more engaging content.

The reality is, you can't afford *not* to be using AI tools.

AI tools aren't here to replace your voice, and they're not going to take your job. They're here to enhance your ability to connect, communicate, and convert more effectively.

Now, I train and coach entrepreneurs, organizations, and corporations on AI, messaging, and brand strategy.

Over time, businesses struggled to integrate AI while staying authentic, so I stepped in to show them how to use technology without losing their voice.

Through my One-on-One Consulting, Done For You Services, and Group Programs, I help business owners:

✦ Build their authority with strategic messaging.

✦ Differentiate themselves in crowded markets.

✦ Use AI to streamline content creation and marketing.

While I'm not currently offering graphic design services, this journey taught me something amazing—sometimes,

Our biggest challenges are divine setups for our next level.

But we have to be brave enough to break the rules and smart enough to do it strategically.

THE POWER OF AUTHENTICITY

As soon as I stopped trying to fit into that "professional business owner" box, my business began to align with who I truly am.

I talking about showing up as my whole self. A Black woman who loves Jesus, rocks sneakers with business casual, and isn't afraid to tell it like it is.

Your quirks are your superpower. Those parts of yourself you've been taught to hide are exactly what make clients remember you, trust you, and choose you over everybody else playing it safe.

I had a VIP client tell me, "Kreda, I hired you because you showed up to our audit call in a v-neck t-shirt and still commanded that call like you were wearing a power suit. You didn't hold anything back."

That wasn't an accident.

It wasn't a branding tactic.

It was me, fully owning who I am.

And when I do that, clients trust me.

I've had private clients work with me because they felt like they could finally drop the "corporate" mask and speak freely. They knew I would help them communicate in a way that felt real and natural, not scripted or robotic, while still professionally challenging conventional ideas.

Because here's the thing…

Authenticity isn't just about being yourself, it's about being intentional with how you show up and connect.

This is why I teach business owners how to use AI tools to refine their voice.

When I started incorporating AI into my messaging work, I wasn't looking for shortcuts. I was using it to enhance my expertise.

AI tools help me see patterns in what my audience responds to the most. They help me structure my content in a way that makes my messaging clearer without losing the heart behind it.

And I'm going to show you exactly how you can make it happen.

AI TOOLS & AUTHENTICITY – YOU CAN HAVE BOTH

When I tell people I use AI in my messaging strategy work, they either assume I'm a tech nerd (which, fair) or that I'm letting robots write all my content.

But here's what they don't get—these tools can help you find what makes your business different. And I love showing skeptics exactly how this looks in real life.

I worked with a VIP client—the owner of an accounting firm— who was drowning in corporate talk. Every word of her marketing sounded like it came from a template: *"comprehensive solutions," "tailored financial strategies," "innovative approaches."*

BOOOOORING!

Every firm in her industry sounded exactly the same.

Using AI-Driven analysis, we found that clients weren't choosing them for their professional tone. They were drawn to them because she had a talent for breaking down complex financial concepts into easy-to-understand language.

That insight changed the game.

Instead of playing corporate "buzzword" bingo, she started sharing real stories about helping clients understand their finances.

Within two months, her LinkedIn following exploded by 300%

But the real win is that she stopped chasing clients because her authentic messaging was doing the work.

She didn't change her voice. She found it.

Here's what makes my approach different. I don't let AI tools take over. I use them as strategic partners, helping me analyze, structure, and create content that connects with your right-fit clients while you focus on your zone of genius and genuine connection.

Here's how I integrate AI into my messaging work:

CHATGPT

My Strategy Bestie — When I need to brainstorm ideas or refine my approach, ChatGPT is my go-to. I use it for outlines, creating full-blown marketing strategies, and analyzing client transcripts from calls which helps me fine-tune their content strategy and identify key themes.

CLAUDE

For Content That Connects — Sometimes your messaging needs to reach people on a deeper level. Its ability to understand nuance and tone helps me create content that stops the scroll and feels natural, more human, and genuinely engaging.

PERPLEXITY

My Research Sidekick — Instead of spending hours digging through articles and links on Google, Perplexity compiles reliable sources, analyzes industry trends, and competitive analysis, and provides insights that allow me to create well-informed, high-value content that positions my clients as industry leaders.

GAMMA

Making It Pretty — For delivering insights in a visually amazing way, Gamma's my go-to to create presentations. Whether I'm preparing for a training session, building a client proposal, or structuring an in-depth workshop, this tool helps me design polished, impactful presentations in minutes—not hours.

WHY I'M SO LOYAL TO THESE TOOLS...

AI tools evolve fast. By the time you read this, new tools will be available, and some of today's favorites might be outdated.

But I test AI tools weekly, and these four continue to show up and show out.

They provide reliable insights, allowing me to base my messaging on real data rather than assumptions. They fit into my workflow like butter, making sure I can focus on strategy without struggling with technology.

I'm intentional about using AI tools responsibly, making sure my messaging is authentic and aligned with my voice and values and rooted in real human connection.

Each of these tools enhances my expertise with clarity, speed and precision while keeping my brand unique and impactful.

HOW YOU CAN MAKE THE MOST OF AI TOOLS

To get the best results from AI tools, you need to understand how to use them strategically.

Master prompting—AI is only as good as the input you give it. The more specific and detailed your prompts, the better the output. AI should never be your final product—it's a starting point. Your creativity and perspective are what make your content stand out.

You also must stay ethical. Be open about using AI tools and make sure everything you create sounds like YOU.

AI tools aren't replacing your voice. They're like your backup singer, helping you hit those high notes, that you can't quite reach, while you stay center stage.

THE FRAMEWORK IN ACTION

If there's one thing I hear over and over again from business owners, it's this: *"I'm not getting quality leads."* They assume it's a visibility problem, but in reality, it's a messaging problem. The right people aren't responding because the messaging isn't speaking directly to them.

Most businesses focus on demographics—age, location, job title, income—but they completely overlook **psychographics** —what their audience thinks, believes, and values. And that's where the real connection happens.

That's why I created my Messaging Alignment Framework— the same step-by-step process I use with my private clients to refine their messaging, attract right-fit clients, and turn engagement into actual business growth.

STEP 1: DEFINE THE OFFER THAT DRIVES THE MESSAGE

Before you create a single post, email, or sales page, you need to get clear on your offer. What problem does it solve? Why should your right-fit clients care? How does it fit into their overall goals and priorities? Your messaging should sell the transformation—not just the service. If your messaging isn't rooted in a clear, compelling offer, everything else will fail.

STEP 2: IDENTIFY YOUR RIGHT-FIT CLIENTS (PSYCHOGRAPHICS & MARKET RESEARCH)

Most business owners get stuck here because they focus too much on job titles and not enough on what drives their clients. Your right-fit clients are not just CEOs or coaches—they are real people with real challenges, values, and priorities.

Psychographics include interests, hobbies, lifestyle choices, values, beliefs, spending habits, and personal goals. And yes, let's be real—you need to know their income level too, because you need to make sure they can afford your offer.

One of the most overlooked ways to do market research? Talk to your past clients. Find out what made them say yes to working with you, what was happening in their life or business before they found you, and what hesitations they had before signing up. AI tools can help, but nothing replaces real conversations with the people who have already invested in you.

STEP 3: AUDIT YOUR CURRENT MESSAGING

Now, it's time to analyze your existing messaging. Is it speaking to the right people? Is it clear, or is it filled with corporate talk and vague language? Is it engaging, or is it blending in with everybody else?

This is where AI can help you audit your own content. Upload your copy into ChatGPT and ask it to act as a messaging strategist. It can analyze whether your messaging is clear, if it aligns with your audience's pain points, and where you're losing engagement. Doing this will help make sure your messaging is clear before you start new content.

STEP 4: USE AI TO ANALYZE WHAT'S WORKING & WHAT'S NOT

At this stage, I use AI to focus on what's already working. Use ChatGPT to analyze engagement data from past content. If you have social media posts, emails, or sales pages that performed well, AI can help pinpoint why they worked and how to replicate that success. This step helps you double down on what's already working instead of wasting time trying to reinvent the wheel.

STEP 5: BUILD A CONTENT & EMAIL MARKETING STRATEGY THAT CONVERTS

Once your messaging is refined, it's time to put it into action with a strategic content plan that positions you as the authority and attracts quality leads. ChatGPT helps map out a marketing and content strategy from transcripts and past trainings, while Claude uses your transcripts to help create content that sounds like you with your emotional appeal. Perplexity helps your messaging stay relevant with up-to-date industry insights. By the end of this step, you'll have a complete messaging system that works across multiple platforms, without spending hours second-guessing what to say.

YOUR AUTHORITY BLUEPRINT

Most business owners think positioning is about standing out, but real authority comes from owning your voice as a strategic thinker and thought leader.

The mistake many make is either hiding their personality completely or letting it spill out with no strategy. Neither works.

Instead, you have to be intentional about how you show up in your industry.

Start by understanding your natural communication style. Are you bold and direct? Funny? A storyteller? A teacher?

Then, ask yourself which industry "rules" you've been following blindly. When have you broken those rules and seen success because of it?

Positioning yourself as a strategic thinker, not just a service provider, starts with how you present your expertise.

How can you make sure your voice isn't just another echo in your industry but one that sparks conversations, challenges perspectives, and shifts mindsets?

For me, my sneakers in business meetings aren't just a fashion choice. After the pandemic, I realized I couldn't rock heels for long anymore. But those sneakers became a visual reminder that you can break the rules and still command respect.

What's your equivalent?

Messaging clarity is about saying the right things to the right people in a way that makes them pay attention and move.

YOUR MESSAGING IS YOUR LEAD MAGNET

If you've been wondering *"Where are my leads?"*—this is it.

They're not ignoring you. They just haven't heard the messaging that makes them stop and say, *"That's exactly what I need."*

Your right-fit clients are searching for someone who speaks their language. And the moment you stop copying and pasting from AI tools and start showing up with clarity, confidence, and strategy, that's when your business starts attracting the leads you've been waiting for.

Make the strategic decision to own your voice, refine your messaging, and position yourself as the authority you already are.

Because when your messaging is clear, the right people take action.

That's how you create impact, build trust, and turn the right audience into loyal, paying clients.

And now, you have the framework to make that happen.

If you're ready to make sure your AI-generated content *actually* sounds like you—and not like every other business owner—take my free AI Voice Audit now. In just 90 seconds, you'll get an AI Voice Analysis Score to see if your content is attracting premium clients or just collecting likes, plus personalized insights and fixes to refine your messaging instantly. Your content should position you as the go-to expert, not blend into the background.

Get your FREE AI Voice Audit now:
https://visionaryvibesolutions.com/aivoiceaudit

ABOUT THE AUTHOR

Kreda McCullough is a Certified Brand Strategist and AI Consultant who specializes in helping busy professionals and business owners gain clarity, achieve alignment, and find success. With a track record of transforming over 300 businesses, Kreda is known for creating messaging systems that generate revenue and connect with the core of their audiences while mirroring their values.

At Visionary Vibe Solutions, she blends strategic insights with a soulful touch, turning challenging ideas into clear, actionable messages that drive results, build trust, and inspire confidence. All while providing the convenience of done-for-you content and strategy solutions, Kreda's approach helps businesses shift from transactional marketing to building meaningful relationships.

For daily insights and actionable strategies that can elevate your brand messaging and accelerate your business growth, connect with Kreda on LinkedIn:

https://linkedin.com/in/kredamccullough.

CHAPTER 5

Making an Impact — The Journey to Authentic Leadership and Empowerment

By Megan Bozzuto

If you asked me to predict 20+ years ago (when I graduated from college) what I'd be doing for a career, I probably would have given you some sort of vague answer about being a leader in corporate America. I would have drawn a perfectly linear line that had me climbing the ladder and progressing through roles while also finding a partner, navigating nuptials, and balancing motherhood. In this vision, I was always "on" and am doing all the things with grace while producing results.

While I have achieved that dream of being a leader in corporate America, the path was nowhere near linear, and the journey has been full of unexpected turns. I get things done and produce results, but I don't usually identify as graceful in the process.

A few years ago (I had already been in my current role as President at the International Association of Women (IAW) for a while), I looked around and thought, *OMG, I'm a leader.* I had the title, and many people looked to me as a leader. But something was missing. I didn't FEEL like a leader. I didn't SEE myself as a leader. I lacked confidence. I lacked boundaries. I definitely wasn't balanced.

And because I didn't feel like a leader, I was failing to make an impact as a leader, and that realization sucked. I had the title but was doing a shit job executing. I was constantly on—putting out fires, saying yes to every request, chasing deliverables, and letting my own self-care fall to the very bottom of my to-do list. I was on the verge of burnout.

So what changed?

I made a decision. I invested in a coach and professional development. I carved out non-negotiable self-care time on my calendar. I set boundaries (and held them). It was only then that I was able to truly step into my role as a leader and have the impact I always wanted. If you're struggling to stand out and have **impact** as a leader, I hope my story will inspire you to make a decision.

IMPACT, in the context of leadership, is the ability to inspire meaningful change, empower others to reach their full potential, and drive results that align with a greater purpose while staying true to your authentic self. It is about leading with intention, prioritizing well-being alongside performance, and fostering a culture of trust and collaboration. True impact emerges when a leader aligns their values, actions, and vision to create a ripple effect that influences not just outcomes but people, teams, and communities.

I – INSPIRATION

Early in my career, I was eager to learn, driven to succeed, and convinced that hard work alone would earn me a seat at the table. I thought that if I put in the effort, delivered results, and proved my capabilities, I would naturally be recognized and given opportunities to grow. But I quickly realized that being qualified wasn't always enough. As a young woman in a male-dominated industry, I often found myself overlooked, dismissed, or underestimated. I watched others—less experienced, less capable—speak up and be heard while I struggled to make my contributions recognized.

The message was clear: my presence in certain spaces wasn't always welcomed, regardless of my expertise. In one role, I was deliberately excluded from meetings with senior leadership because one of the men in the room was known to be crass, and women were often offended by his comments. Instead of addressing the real issue—his behavior—the solution was to remove women from the conversation altogether. I was told that my presence in that room was a *lawsuit waiting to happen*. My ability to contribute was overshadowed by the discomfort others had in holding one of their own accountable.

In another role, I walked into a meeting fully prepared to lead the discussion, confident in my knowledge and expertise. But as I scanned the room filled with middle-aged white men, my confidence quickly met resistance. Before I could even introduce myself, the leader of the group scoffed and said, *"What could you possibly tell us about this topic?"* His words dismissed me before I even had the chance to speak. In that moment, I felt small—like all my preparation and experience didn't matter simply because of how I looked.

These experiences could have broken me. They could have forced me into silence, made me question my worth, or led me to believe that I didn't belong in these spaces. And for a while, I did question myself. I second-guessed my knowledge, my abilities, and whether I even wanted to keep pushing forward in environments that weren't built for me.

But here's the thing: I *did* belong in those rooms. I *did* have valuable insights to share. And I refused to let outdated mindsets dictate my future. Instead of letting these moments define me, I let them fuel me. I decided that if the system wasn't going to make space for me, I would create space for myself—and for other women who deserved to be seen, heard, and valued.

Leadership isn't just about being the loudest voice in the room. It's about knowing your worth, standing firm in your expertise, and refusing to shrink yourself to fit into spaces that weren't designed with you in mind. My journey has taught me that the biggest barriers aren't always about skill or intelligence—they're about breaking through the invisible walls that others put in front of you. And once you do, you clear the path for those who come after you.

> **Tip:** Reflect on your journey and identify the moments where you felt undervalued or overlooked. Ask yourself: How can these experiences inspire you to lead with empathy, inclusivity, and a commitment to creating spaces where others can succeed? The lessons in adversity often become the seeds of our greatest impact.

M – MENTORSHIP

For a long time, I felt completely alone in my professional journey. I was surrounded by colleagues and friends, but the thought of speaking up felt like tattling. I didn't want to rock the boat, and asking for help seemed like admitting weakness. So, I pushed through on my own, bottling up my frustrations. I vented to my mom often, but over time, resentment started creeping in, tainting everything I once enjoyed about my career.

Here's the truth: Nobody has to navigate their journey alone. You can try to go it solo, but there's immense power in seeking support.

Asking for help isn't easy— it requires vulnerability and courage— but it's essential for growth.

When I finally tapped into the power of mentorship, everything changed. I realized that admitting what you don't know isn't a sign of weakness—it's the first step toward getting better. Having a trusted mentor to guide and support me made the process of growth not just manageable but empowering.

Mentorship isn't just about being mentored, though. It's a two-way street. One of the most rewarding things you can do is raise your hand to mentor others. Investing your time and energy into someone else's success not only strengthens their journey but enriches yours as well. When we lift each other up, we all achieve more.

Tip: Don't wait for mentorship to find you—take the initiative. Whether you're seeking guidance or offering it, start by identifying people whose experiences or perspectives align with your goals. Reach out, build connections, and remember: Mentorship is about mutual growth, not perfection.

P – PURPOSE

For much of my career, I saw success as a ladder to climb—a series of milestones, promotions, and accomplishments. I poured my energy into developing my skills, enhancing my network, and achieving tangible results. But somewhere along the way, I realized I was running on autopilot. While I was achieving success by traditional standards, I wasn't fulfilled. My work felt transactional, and I found myself yearning for something deeper—a connection between what I was doing and who I wanted to be.

The turning point came when I decided to step back and ask the hard questions: What do I value most? What kind of impact do I want to have in the world? How can I align my work with my purpose? These questions led me to pivot from a tactical role to one that focused on strategy and purpose-driven outcomes.

This shift wasn't just about career growth—it was about creating a life and legacy that aligned with my core values. I found clarity in knowing that my purpose is rooted in empowering others, fostering authentic leadership, and building inclusive communities. Now, every decision I make—professionally and personally—stems from that foundation.

Purpose isn't just a guiding principle; it's the fuel that keeps me focused and energized.

Tip: To uncover your purpose, start by reflecting on your values, your passions, and the impact you want to have on others. Ask yourself: What energizes me? What legacy do I want to leave? Then, align your goals with that purpose. Remember, a purpose-driven life doesn't just happen—it's built intentionally, one decision at a time.

A – AUTHENTICITY

The word *authenticity* gets tossed around so much these days that it's easy to overlook its true meaning. Social media is often a stage for perfectly curated lives, leaving little room for the messiness of reality. Yet, ironically, it's the mess that often creates the most meaningful impact.

There was a time when I was perfectly content staying behind the scenes. The thought of showing up as my true self was terrifying. What if people judged me? What if they didn't like me? Worse, what if they discovered I wasn't as capable as they thought? (Hello, Imposter Syndrome!)

But here's the truth: We're all human. And when we show up authentically—embracing our imperfections—we create connections. Those connections build trust, the foundation of any meaningful relationship, professional or personal.

As President of IAW, I've had to step into the spotlight more often than I ever imagined. Whether I'm moderating live panels or speaking at virtual events, I'm front and center with the IAW community. I'll never forget the first time I shared something deeply personal—I was navigating a divorce. I was hesitant and worried about being judged or viewed differently. But the response was remarkable. Instead of judgment, I received empathy, support, and connection like never before.

What I've learned is this: Everyone has insecurities, challenges, and messes in their lives. Authenticity doesn't mean sharing every detail of your struggles, but it does mean letting your humanity shine through. When you lead with humility and allow others a glimpse into your story, you create a powerful bond of trust and understanding.

Tip: Start practicing authenticity by sharing small, personal insights in appropriate settings. Reflect on moments in your journey where vulnerability could foster connection. Try this exercise: Write down three things you're comfortable sharing about your challenges or growth. Use these moments as a bridge to build trust with your team, colleagues, or community.

C – COURAGE

Comfort zones are like cozy, warm spaces—a refuge of safety and predictability. But they can also become prisons that keep us from reaching our full potential.

There was a time in my career when I was terrified to speak up in meetings. I'd sit in the back of the room, diligently taking notes, nodding in agreement, and brainstorming brilliant ideas in my head—but never raising my hand to share them. Looking back now, I realize how my lack of courage held me back. Those unspoken ideas, those moments of hesitation, were missed opportunities to contribute, grow, and be seen.

The truth is, if you want to excel, you must step outside your comfort zone—and not just once, but often. Courage isn't a trait you're born with; it's a skill you build through experience.

Think about it: If a year from now, you're still in the same place because fear kept you from taking risks, will you regret it? If someone else gets the promotion or opportunity you know you deserved simply because you were too afraid to raise your voice, will you look back and wish you had acted differently?

The moment I began raising my hand, sharing ideas, and taking risks, I started achieving more. But not just that; it also sparked a shift in those around me. My courage became the catalyst for others to step out of their own comfort zones.

As leaders, this is one of the most powerful tools we have for cultivating talent. When we demonstrate courage, we create a culture where others feel empowered to contribute their best ideas, take risks, and embrace challenges. It's a ripple effect—your bravery encourages someone else to try, and before you know it, you've built a team of bold, innovative thinkers.

Courage grows incrementally. It starts with small steps—asking a question, offering an idea, or saying "Yes" to a challenge. Each step builds confidence, preparing you for the bigger leaps that will truly transform your journey.

> **Tip:** Stretch your courage muscle by committing to one small, bold action each week. It could be volunteering to lead a project, sharing an idea in a meeting, or reaching out to a mentor. Reflect on the outcome and celebrate the progress, no matter how small. Remember, courage isn't about fearlessness—it's about acting despite the fear.

T – TRANSFORMATION

When I think back to my 22-year-old self entering corporate America, I'm in awe of the journey that has shaped who I am today, both professionally and personally. At that time, I had a picture-perfect vision of success: the corner office, the fancy car, financial security, perfect health, and a happy family.

What I couldn't have predicted were the twists and turns that would define the road from there to here. Both the challenges and the opportunities have been unexpected, and they've completely reshaped how I view success. Today, success for me isn't about external symbols—it's about the *impact* I create for myself, my family, and others.

Stepping into a leadership role where I could make a meaningful impact didn't happen overnight. It required transformation—both in mindset and in action. I had to:

✦ Gain clarity on my *core values* and what they truly mean to me.

✦ Define my *WHY*—the deeper motivation that drives me to show up every day.

✦ Let go of beliefs and expectations that were no longer serving me.

✦ Prioritize my own needs as non-negotiables to sustain my energy and focus.

✦ Set and maintain firm *boundaries* to protect my time, health, and well-being.

Transformation isn't a single event; it's a series of intentional choices. It's about evolving into the best version of yourself, not by chasing an external image of success but by aligning with your values, purpose, and vision for the impact you want to make.

> **Tip:** Start your transformation by reflecting on your current definition of success. Ask yourself: Does this align with my values and long-term goals? Identify one limiting belief or habit that's holding you back, and create an action plan to release it. Remember, transformation begins with clarity and the courage to take the first step.

MAKING AN IMPACT

As you've read this chapter, I hope you've found inspiration, tools, and encouragement to step into your authentic leadership and embrace the impact you're meant to make. Each section—Inspiration, Mentorship, Purpose, Authenticity, Courage, and Transformation—has been a piece of the puzzle, guiding you toward becoming the best version of yourself.

Here's what I want you to take away:

- ✦ **Inspiration**: Your story and experiences hold incredible value. When you reflect on where you've been and what has shaped you, you can find the spark to move forward with purpose and determination. Inspiration is often rooted in the unexpected moments that define our paths.

✦ **Mentorship**: None of us can do this alone. Mentorship —both giving and receiving—is a cornerstone of growth. Surround yourself with people who challenge, support, and inspire you, and pay it forward by mentoring others. Together, we can all achieve more.

✦ **Purpose**: True success comes when you align your actions with your values and a deeper sense of purpose. Knowing your "why" gives you clarity, motivation, and focus. Purposeful leadership isn't about titles or accolades; it's about creating a life of meaning and impact.

✦ **Authenticity**: The world doesn't need perfection—it needs real, human connection. By showing up as your authentic self, with vulnerability and humility, you create trust and build stronger relationships. Authenticity is the foundation for lasting influence and leadership.

✦ **Courage**: Growth requires stepping outside of your comfort zone, time and time again. Courage isn't about fearlessness; it's about taking action despite the fear. When you lead with courage, you empower others to do the same, creating a ripple effect of confidence and innovation.

✦ **Transformation**: Becoming a leader who makes an impact requires intentional growth. It means redefining success, letting go of what no longer serves you, and aligning your life with your values. Transformation is an ongoing journey built on clarity, resilience, and a commitment to continuous improvement.

You are capable of making a profound impact—not just in your career but in your community, your family, and the lives of those around you. The journey won't always be easy, and the path may not be linear, but every step forward brings you closer to the leader you're meant to be.

YOUR NEXT STEP:

I challenge you to take one immediate action that aligns with the principles of IMPACT. Whether it's seeking out a mentor, setting a bold new goal, or simply reflecting on your core values, let this be the beginning of your next chapter.

Remember: Leadership isn't about having all the answers—it's about showing up, learning, and growing every single day. You've got this. Now, go out and make your impact.

And if you need a nudge of encouragement or somebody on your side, find me on LinkedIn and get in touch.

ABOUT THE AUTHOR

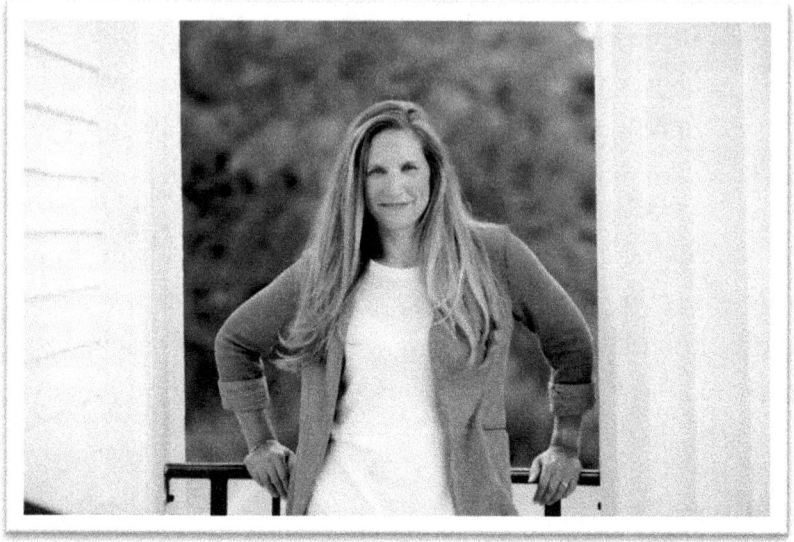

Megan Bozzuto is a dynamic leader and strategic innovator, currently serving as the Interim Chief Financial Officer of Professional Diversity Inc. (PDN) and President of the International Association of Women (IAW). With over 20 years of experience spanning Accounting, Finance, and Marketing, Megan has held many influential roles and has been instrumental in empowering women and fostering growth through inclusive leadership.

Since joining IAW in 2017, Megan has played a pivotal role in shaping its mission and impact, combining her expertise in strategy, mentorship, and authentic leadership. Her career journey reflects her commitment to building thriving, inclusive communities and fostering human-first leadership.

A proud global citizen, Megan has lived and worked across the U.S., Shanghai, and Dubai, gaining a broad perspective that informs her leadership approach. She holds a Bachelor of Science in Accounting Information Systems from Bentley University and currently resides in the Boston area with her three children.

Megan is dedicated to making an IMPACT—leading with Inspiration, Mentorship, Purpose, Authenticity, Courage, and Transformation—and empowering others to do the same.

Connect with Megan on LinkedIn.

https://www.linkedin.com/in/megbozz/

CHAPTER 6

Reclaiming Your Financial Power

By Micah James

As many of us do from time to time, moments of reflection allow us to take account of the wins, losses, and lessons in our lives. When it comes to money, many of us struggle to have an honest conversation about what money is, how it makes us feel, and where money gets its power. In our short time together in this chapter, we will take a moment to reflect on each of these questions. By reflecting on these questions, my goal is for you to gain insight into your relationship with money. By the end of this chapter, you will have a clearer idea about your history with money, your values around money, and your control over your money (or its control over you).

WHAT IS IT?

Money is such a strange thing. We put value in a piece of paper or plastic to exchange for the items or services we need or want daily. But at the end of the day, what is money? Money is not paper or plastic; money is the tool we use to exchange resources. When resource exchange began as bartering, we were much more closely connected to the resource we were giving up in exchange for what resource we were receiving. For example, a person would exchange lumber for sugar or animal pelts for vegetables. You could clearly see what you were giving up and receiving in these exchanges. The onus was on both parties to ensure a fair deal was being negotiated.

In our modern system, we are much further removed from the things being exchanged. On the surface, we are exchanging dollars and cents for an item, but really we are not. We are trading our time, talent, and skill for that particular item or service which results from someone else's time, talent, and skill, which we often never know or meet.

When we stop for a moment and consider what we are really exchanging, it may cause us to slow down and consider the value of the item or service we are purchasing in a different light. Is it worth exchanging four hours of work for a meal at a restaurant? Is it worth exchanging a week's worth of work for a new gaming console? Only you can determine this, but it is worth pausing to consider. You have a finite amount of time and so you have a finite amount of resources to support yourself with.

Exchanging the equivalent hours of time or skill allows us to assess the value of items differently. Take a moment to reflect on your understanding of what money is and how you relate to it.

Reflection Questions

✦ When and how did you first learn about money?

✦ What did you learn about money from your family of origin?

✦ How have those lessons guided your understanding of what money is or does and what it isn't and doesn't do?

HOW MONEY MAKES US FEEL

Understanding that money is an exchange of resources is only one part of the equation. One of the biggest challenges when it comes to gaining control of our finances is wrestling with our feelings about money. These feelings may come from our historical experiences in our family of origin, our first experiences with our money management, or even our feelings about how things are currently going. At times, some of the most significant negative emotions and feelings—shame, guilt, unworthiness, and anxiety—are triggered or amplified by our usage of money.

Emotions cloud our ability to make clear and wise decisions. When we are in a heightened emotional state, we focus on resolving or escaping the pain, discomfort, or stress we're feeling as quickly as possible. This focus on resolving feelings is not the space for making financial decisions while escaping them just delays the inevitable decisions that need to be made. To make wise financial decisions, our minds cannot be swayed by options that resolve these feelings quickly but not to our long-term benefit. We need to be able to weigh all options carefully and thoughtfully even if making hard choices leads to temporary financial pain or stress.

One of the greatest gifts we offer our clients in coaching is a low-emotion perspective in a safe space to share openly and confidentially. Sometimes, it is challenging to disconnect your money (and the things you need your money to do for you) from your feelings about it. When you can assess the perspective on your resources previously discussed from a low-emotion perspective, seeing them as the outgrowth of your time, talents, and skills, you regain your power over your finances.

Feelings are powerful and can be both positive and negative, depending on how we use them. They can draw us off-center to the mountaintop highs and the melancholy lows. When we let our negative feelings about money guide our decisions, we will constantly be tossed up and down, side to side. We have to be centered and focused on our values when making financial decisions, and this comes when we truly understand that we are in control. Martin Luther King Jr. once said, "Your budget is a moral document," meaning it reflects your values and what you choose to prioritize in living out your life. We need to live our lives in alignment with our core values to thrive and reach our goals.

Reflection Questions

✦ What is your earliest memory of purchasing with your own money? How did it make you feel?

✦ Do you make different financial choices when you are emotional? If so, when does this happen, and what do you do differently?

✦ How can you create a low-emotion environment in which to discuss your finances? How can you ensure your financial decisions align with who you are?

✦ Where does money get its power?

As a person of Christian faith, one of the scriptures I have wrestled with is Matthew 6:24. This scripture is often used in conversations around stewardship and charity. The scripture says, "No one can serve two masters; for either he will hate the one and love the other, or he will be devoted to the one and despise the other. You cannot serve God and mammon." Mammon is a Semitic word for money or riches. Some Christians would interpret this as saying that serving money is a selfish act that takes one's focus off of serving and loving others, which is God's call in our lives. As I have wrestled with this scripture, the word that I have come back to over and over again is stewardship.

Power is critical to understand as we consider money and how it makes us feel.

Stewardship is not the first word that most think of when they define power. The historic concept of stewardship arose during medieval times, when a person would manage the estate and resources of the noble person they served for the benefit of all parties. The more modern understanding of steward might have you thinking of a staff member on a boat or restaurant. As I have spent many years studying what it means to be a steward, I have embraced the idea that being a steward is having a caretaker stance with your finances. Adding this to our definition of power allows us to empower ourselves to be in charge of our finances without measuring our value from it.

When we derive our value from the amount of money or things we have, we allow something outside ourselves to determine our worth. This serves to deemphasize our innate value and worth as a human being. This determination of self-value based on money allows, just like feelings, our value to get tossed about with the value of our financial portfolio. When we take a steward or caretaker stance, our value is in the choices we make, the values we hold, and the service we provide. This stance allows for a more steady approach because even when our bank account balance is low, our choices, values, and service to our family and community can remain constant. The only adjustment is the scale.

Money gains its power based on the way we use it in our lives. If we are using money to determine our worth, money can make us feel worthy or worthless. When we give money that kind of power, our worth will always be at the mercy of the inescapable things that come with life. The power is shifted when we look at money as one of many resources in our care. You reclaim your power because you can ground your value in things you control, such as your values, choices, and actions. Ultimately, your value is more profound than anything you do; you are valuable because you are you. You are not valuable because you did something correct or have enough resources. When you understand your more profound value, not connected to a bank balance, you will achieve the grandest power—self-confidence, self-worth, and assuredness that you are living the life you truly want.

Reflection Questions

✦ How do you understand the power of money?

✦ Do you allow the amount of money you have to impact your value?

✦ How can you take a more steward stance toward your finances?

PERSONAL JOURNEY TO RECLAIM MY FINANCIAL POWER

My journey to financial health is a winding one. Admittedly, I didn't arrive at these conclusions overnight. I have been on a long journey of these discoveries. Anyone who meets me knows that I am a BIG feeler—full of passion, love, and (yes) anxiety. This tendency to put my feelings before my strategy was how I navigated most of my early money management years. What this led to was saying yes to a lot of things I should have said no to. Like most, I didn't make much money in my early professional years, but that didn't mean that the world automatically adjusted to my income level. Invitations to go out to eat still came, opportunities to attend events with friends popped up, and the latest tech was always just a run to Target away. In addition, my big feeling heart could never say no to an invitation to give five dollars here and there to local non-profits raising funds for their latest initiative. My early understanding of stewardship was one of sacrifice, leaving my needs unmet. In the end, I had more stress, more guilt, and less stability than I wanted. My heart was doing the financial planning, not my brain.

Over the years, I have attempted to change my situation through education. I believed if I read more books and attended more seminars, it would fix my struggles. I learned a lot over that time, but ultimately, I needed a behavioral change, not just a knowledge change. This is when I dived into understanding being a steward and what it really meant to care for the resources in my care.

In this quest to reframe my financial management, I knew I could not do this alone. As a former high school athlete, I knew the best way to stick to a new (or complex) discipline practice was to find a coach. I didn't know what a coach for your money looked like then, but I knew I needed someone to see the bigger picture, remove the emotion, and hold the plan steady until I could hold it myself.

The first meeting with my financial coach was a tough one. I wanted to get an "A" on my financial plan, but I knew going into the meeting that I was on this path because I was definitely not there yet. The first full sharing of your finances is one of the most intense feelings of vulnerability I believe one can feel. If you have never really laid out all the good, the bad, and the ugly of what is happening in your finances—without holding anything back—the experience can be terrifying and liberating. By the end of my first meeting with my financial coach, I was overwhelmed. I had laid my whole financial world out in front of her, and now my question was, "Now what?" Like any good teacher or mentor, my financial coach didn't give me the answers. The answer to that question was now up to me. With each subsequent meeting, she gave me a little more of the framework and a little more push to answer what I wanted my financial life to look like. I spent the next three months learning how to budget, managing my stress, embracing a stewardship perspective, and internalizing that all I can do is all I can do. One step at a time in the same direction will, over time, lead to a full-blown journey.

When I said I internalized the phrase "All I can do is all I can do," it was the key to connecting what money is, how money makes me feel, and understanding money's power in my life. This was at the core of my movement to live as a steward of my resources. At some point in my life, I had internalized the notion of giving 110% at everything. It is a common motivating sentiment—"Give your 110%." But if you break that down, there is no way you can do that. Internalizing this notion happened to me because I always thought there was more I could do, give, or be. By owning the mantra, "All I can do is all I can do," I became content that my hardest work was being the best caretaker of my resources at this moment and time. By being the best steward of my resources, I was doing all I could. This idea helped me clearly communicate my financial boundaries because when the money is gone, the spending is done.

The skills and mindset I learned in coaching required daily practice and regular resets. Coaching was not a magic potion but a way of planting seeds I could water into fruitful practices over time.

CHALLENGE

We all have a choice regarding our finances—to let it control us or to empower ourselves. My journey to empowerment has offered me so many challenges and experiences to learn along the way. Through the reflection questions in this chapter, you have the opportunity to gain some understanding of the power of money in your life. To continue this exploration with us, Empowering Financial Coaching offers you a FREE resource. Go to www.empoweringfinancialcoaching.com/free to take the next step on your journey of discovery and empowerment. It's time to reclaim your financial power!

ABOUT THE AUTHOR

Micah James serves as the Chief Empowerment Officer (CEO) of Empowering Financial Coaching, LLC, bringing a wealth of experience from her background in education, ministry, and coaching. With a degree in Education and a Master of Divinity, she has honed her ability to engage diverse learning styles, offer compassionate support, and lead teams with purpose. Her professional journey, driven by a passion for helping others, includes earning her CFRE (Certified Fundraising Executive) certification, reflecting her ongoing commitment to excellence.

Inspired by her own financial challenges and triumphs—and the support that made a difference—Micah co-founded Empowering Financial Coaching alongside her partner, Charles Roberts. Together, they are dedicated to serving as accountability partners and cheerleaders for their clients. Their coaching program is designed to help individuals and families discover personalized strategies to achieve financial empowerment and lasting success.

Enjoy FREE resources from Empowering Financial Coaching at empoweringfinancialcoaching.com/free

CHAPTER 7

The Influential Woman Effect

By Dr. Christi Monk Andrews

In today's world, societal norms can profoundly impact the roles women play, professionally and personally. Reflecting on my personal journey, I am reminded of the times I played it safe, rescued others who did not need to be rescued, functioned in codependency, and failed to set the necessary boundaries in all areas of my life. To be frank, I was a performer and a people pleaser. It wasn't until I faced the significant personal and professional decision of quitting my six-figure job that I realized I was not being true to myself. I was living up to everyone else's expectations but not my own.

A few therapy sessions opened my eyes to a hard truth—I wasn't living in alignment with my core values. In fact, I didn't even know what they were. I didn't understand how vital core values were to creating a fulfilled life on my terms.

Now, you may be in a similar space: earning a great salary or holding multiple degrees and certifications but feeling like all of it is just a way to overcompensate for a deeper need for external validation—something that likely happens more often than you realize.

I am the second child, but the oldest girl—a role that came with its own set of responsibilities. Growing up, I was the one tasked with looking after my siblings. At first, it felt like an honor—a badge of trust and importance. But over time, that sense of pride shifted into something heavier.

By the time I was an adult, I had mastered the art of holding it all together. Crying? Not an option. Showing emotion? A luxury I couldn't afford. I had to focus on getting things done, no matter what. I became the leader—the thinker, the planner, the one who always had the answers. I told others what to do, how to do it, and made sure it all got done.

That's where I picked up a habit that would follow me into adulthood: control. I controlled everything—every detail, every decision. But this control didn't stay confined to just my responsibilities. It spilled over into my relationships, especially with men. Let's just say that's a chapter best saved for another book.

My transformation began the moment I was confronted with a profound and unsettling truth: my discomfort with vulnerability—something I once saw as a weakness—was standing in the way of my personal growth. Beneath the surface, I carried a silent regret for not speaking up, for not expressing my needs when it mattered most.

Instead of asserting my boundaries or simply saying "No," I often chose the path of least resistance, doing what others expected of me. Frustration simmered inside me, yet my relentless desire to appear strong kept me from sharing my true feelings. Vulnerability felt risky and exposing, and I feared it might shatter the image I had built of being unshakable.

Eventually, I reached a point where I began questioning everything: *Why am I here? What is my true purpose?*

Sometimes, it felt easier to just walk away—to leave situations or relationships without addressing the unspoken truths. But deep down, I knew that avoiding discomfort was holding me back from the authentic connections and growth I so deeply craved. This is why I developed the *Influential Woman Effect*.

The *Influential Woman Effect* is the transformative power a woman embodies when she aligns her life with her core values, embraces her authentic self, and confidently steps into her role as a leader of her own life resulting in fulfillment and satisfaction, personally and professionally.

Becoming an influential woman is a journey that unfolds in six clear steps. First, you must live by your core values so you learn to make yourself a priority. This will empower you to communicate assertively, which is crucial for managing expectations and establishing clear boundaries. Once you've mastered these four steps, you'll be well-equipped to effectively resolve conflicts and, ultimately, develop and cultivate healthy relationships.

Living by your core values is not just a practice, it's a source of empowerment.

It brings a profound sense of clarity, confidence, and direction to your life. It guides you to make decisions that resonate with your true self, leading to a more fulfilling and authentic life. When your core values are clearly defined, you can navigate challenges, set appropriate bound-aries, and build resilience. This empowerment is the key to your personal and professional growth.

Many of us learn our core values from the influential people in our lives. Some may be good, and others questionable. When you think about your core values, how were yours defined? This reminds me of a story where the ends of a ham were cut off before it was put in the oven. Over time, that became a family tradition, but when the first person to do it was asked why it was done that way, they simply replied, "The ham was too big for my pan." Every action, reaction, and belief you exhibit carries the imprint of what you've observed. Whether it's the way you communicate, how you handle conflict, or the way you navigate vulnerability—these learned patterns play a significant role in how you connect with and influence others.

Now ask yourself: Are these habits aligned with the person you want to be, or is it time to unlearn and rewrite them? True influence begins when we consciously choose behaviors that reflect our values and our vision rather than remaining stuck in the patterns of the past.

Think back to that one relationship or the last job that left you feeling utterly drained, annoyed, and frustrated. You know the one—the situation where walking away or quitting seemed like the best option, yet you stayed. Maybe it was because you saw the potential for change in the person, believing you could fix them. Or perhaps it was the allure of a higher paycheck that kept you locked in place.

But despite all the effort you poured in, prioritizing their needs over your own, you were left feeling unfulfilled. The love, appreciation, or recognition you thought you had earned never came. Instead, you found yourself stuck in a cycle of giving, hoping, and waiting—only to realize that no amount of sacrifice could fill the void left by neglecting yourself.

Once you've identified your core values, something powerful begins to happen—you learn to prioritize yourself. This becomes the foundation for personal growth and lasting fulfillment. But before you can fully embrace this shift, you must first recognize what it looks and feels like when you *don't* prioritize yourself.

It's in the moments when you say "Yes" to others but "No" to your own needs. It's the exhaustion that creeps in when you overextend yourself to meet everyone else's expectations. It's the frustration of feeling unseen or unappreciated, even after giving so much. And it's the quiet realization that you've been putting yourself last for far too long.

Acknowledging this is the first step. Only then can you break free from the cycle and start building a life that aligns with who you truly are and what matters most to you. Prioritizing yourself isn't selfish—it's the ultimate act of self-respect. When you prioritize yourself, you not only thrive but also inspire those around you to do the same.

By putting yourself first, you build the emotional resilience needed to face life's challenges with strength and clarity. This self-prioritization becomes the foundation for effective communication—the sweet spot known as assertive communication. It's the balance between standing firm in your truth and respecting others, creating connections that are both honest and empowering.

When you do not communicate assertively, you may appear indecisive, overly accommodating, or even dismissive of your needs. Your confidence can become diminished, impacting your self-esteem and leading to feeling frustrated or resenting others. You might even believe your opinions do not matter. Having a lack of assertiveness can have you being consistently overlooked for opportunities or feeling dismissed.

Assertive communication empowers you to confidently express your thoughts and feelings clearly and professionally, leaving little room for misinterpretation. You stay calm in difficult situations, address issues constructively, and take responsibility for your actions. You master saying "No" without guilt, focus on solutions over problems, and embrace feedback as an opportunity to grow.

Assertive communication is key to managing expectations, a vital skill for any woman striving to embody the influential woman effect. Too often, we carry unspoken expectations of others while letting them place unrealistic demands on us. The root? Two common challenges: struggling to say "No" and the ever-present superwoman complex—the belief that we can save the world.

You know you're not managing expectations when you let last-minute requests disrupt your plans, fail to set clear boundaries, or overcommit and rush to meet deadlines. Burnout sets in, leaving you isolated as you strive to maintain a perfect image of getting everything done. I call this the *Flawless Female Syndrome*. Avoiding conflict and neglecting to communicate limitations are clear signs that expectations are managing you instead of the other way around.

Effectively managing expectations boosts your credibility and strengthens your influence in decision-making. It ensures you don't overpromise or underdeliver, enabling you to communicate realistically and follow through consistently. By balancing others' needs with your capabilities, you set boundaries, reduce stress, and prevent burnout. Managing expectations also lays the groundwork for handling conflict constructively, creating a stronger foundation for success.

Effective conflict management is essential for building and maintaining healthy relationships. Unresolved issues can lead to mistrust, resentment, and even a toxic workplace culture, with costly consequences for both individuals and organizations. Avoiding conflict often signals passive-aggressive tendencies and worsens the situation over time.

You know you've mastered conflict management when you understand your conflict resolution style and see improvements in your relationships. By using emotional intelligence to regulate your emotions and recognize your role, you can address conflicts promptly and respectfully. Speaking to the facts and addressing the behavior causing the issue fosters understanding and resolution. This approach paves the way for healthy relationships—something every woman strives for.

Establishing healthy relationships is the cornerstone for personal empowerment and professional success. I always say,

"You can't go professionally where you are unwilling to go personally." The quality of our relationships as women can either elevate us or hold us back from reaching our full potential. Your relationships serve as the foundation for establishing community and expanding your influence to make a lasting impact in the world.

> Take inventory of your relationships. Are they adding to you or draining you? Are you able to be your authentic self in the relationship? Do you accept each other's flaws? Are you comfortable sharing your thoughts and feelings without being defensive or feeling someone will judge you?

Have you taken the time to assess your core values, make yourself a priority, and learn the art of communicating assertively so that you can manage expectations and address conflict to establish healthy relationships? If the answer to any of these questions is no, here are six steps to experiencing the influential woman effect.

1. **Define and Live by Your Core Values**. Take time to identify your core values. You should establish your core values in five key areas: work, home and personal environment, intimate relationships, family, and friends/social life. Question traditions and beliefs like the "ham story"—are these traditions serving you, or are they just habits? Create a personal mission

statement aligned with these values and use it as a compass for decision-making.

2. **Master the Art of Self-Prioritization**. Start by blocking dedicated time for self-care and personal development in your calendar and treat these appointments as non-negotiable. Address signs of self-neglect like unused gym memberships, abandoned hobbies, or postponed personal goals. Monitor your energy levels and learn to recognize when you're operating from depletion rather than abundance.

3. **Learn to Communicate Assertively**. Express your thoughts without over-explaining or making excuses. Train yourself to pause and assess your mental and emotional capacity before saying "Yes" to requests. Work on maintaining a calm, steady tone even in challenging conversations. Learn to share your perspective without hesitation. Be open to feedback. Ask questions. Actively listen for understanding, not to respond. Ask for help if you need it.

4. **Manage Expectations**. Create clear communication protocols for both personal and professional relation-ships. Set realistic timelines for commitments and learn to say "No" to last-minute requests that overrule your plans. Document agreements and deadlines to prevent misunderstandings. Hold others accountable.

5. **Build Your Conflict Resolution Skills**. Practice self-awareness to develop emotional intelligence. Address issues promptly rather than letting them linger or avoiding them altogether. Focus on the behaviors you want to address rather than personal attacks. Learn your conflict resolution style and use it effectively while remaining open to understanding others' perspectives.

6. **Create Healthy Relationship Standards**. Regularly evaluate your relationships by reflecting on key questions: Does this person add value to your life or drain your energy? Can you show up as your authentic self? Is there mutual acceptance and respect? Have you clearly established and consistently communicated your boundaries? Foster vulnerability by being open and honest while firmly maintaining your boundaries. This balance is the cornerstone of healthy, fulfilling connections.

Are you ready to step into the *Influential Woman Effect*? I'm here to guide you on this transformative journey. Visit www.christimonk.com and select **Work with Dr. Christi** to schedule your personalized strategy session. My mission is to help you STAY true to who you are.

When you embrace the *Influential Woman Effect*, you:

✦ **Stand** in your power unapologetically.

✴ **Take** control of your thoughts and actions.

✴ **Assess** whose support you need to succeed.

✴ **Yield** to the woman you were always meant to be.

Let's unlock the powerful, authentic you—together.

ABOUT THE AUTHOR

Dr. Christi Monk-Andrews is a two-time best-selling author, Life Coach, and distinguished multicultural consultant with over 25 years of expertise in Organizational Development, Change Management, Conflict Resolution, and Workplace Mediation. Her methodology uniquely combines Emotional Intelligence and the Core Values System, advocating for a deeper understanding of differences to foster cultural shifts and improve performance. Dr. Christi's approach has established her as a key figure in creating safe spaces for candid conversations, helping individuals and organizations enhance connectedness and minimize conflicts. Leveraging her life's journey, personally and professionally, she is the founder of the Dr. Christi Experience, which specializes in supporting women on how to properly set boundaries in all areas of their lives to STAY true to themselves by training them how to Stand in their power unapologetically, Take control of their thoughts and actions, Assess whose help they need so they can Yield to the authenticity of the woman they were created to be. As a result, her clients become BOLD. They learn to Be their best selves, Operate fully in their gifts and talents, and Live their best lives so they can Dare to be different. She calls this the Influential Woman Effect.

CHAPTER 8

From Medicine to Adventure — A Fulfilling Medical Career

By Deborah Jenkins

I had an amazing medical career, including almost 13 years of outreach with Doctors Without Borders. That work took me to eight different countries, some French-speaking, where I used the French I had studied in high school. To prepare, I studied travel medicine and earned a certificate in public health. Over time, I went from anesthesiology to managing small hospital medical staff. It was adventurous and fulfilling, and I loved helping people, but being away from the States for so long wasn't easy.

LIFE AFTER OUTREACH

After 13 years of travel, I reached a crossroads. I could've traveled, settled in a French-speaking country, tutored math and science, or just relaxed like many retired friends. The possibilities were exciting but also overwhelming.

Ultimately, I decided to stay closer to home to spend more time with my elderly mom. The loss of an elderly friend who had been like a second mother to me was a stark reminder of how short life really is. So, I chose to stay in Tulsa, Oklahoma, the family home. It just felt like the right time to focus on family.

REUNITING THROUGH FACEBOOK

Out of the blue, in the spring of 2014, my brother asked me, "Do you remember Julius Warren?" I was taken aback. Of course, I remembered my high school sweetheart and two-time prom date. The unexpected mention of his name brought a rush of memories and emotions and a sense of excitement at the prospect of rekindling a past relationship.

I hadn't heard from Julius in over 35 years. Usually, in middle age, when someone asks, "Do you remember so-and-so?" It's followed by sad news like a stroke, a heart attack, cancer, or a retirement party I'd missed. But this time, my brother said, "Julius is my new Facebook friend." I pretended not to be surprised or interested in this news. Why would it matter that my brother had a new Facebook friend? I waited a few hours to look at Julius' Facebook page. Curiosity was natural. Right?

At first, I hardly recognized him—he looked old. Well, so was I! It was when he smiled that I saw the Julius I knew. I was missing a few details about the new Facebook friend. My brother and Julius' nephew had recently attended a conference and appeared together in several photos. Julius deliberately befriended my brother on Facebook to see my profile. I messaged him, he messaged back, and over the past ten years, there hasn't been a single day since that we haven't talked or spent time together. If this were a movie, it would be titled *High School Sweethearts Find Love Again Through Facebook.*

TURNING DREAMS INTO REALITY: BUILDING THE BUSINESS

Julius worked as a senior technician for a large HVAC company in Atlanta. We maintained a long-distance relationship over the next five years, with me spending several weeks in both locations. Julius often shared his dream of returning to Tulsa and reopening his heating and air conditioning business.

As Julius reminisced about his days of owning his own company, I listened intently, drawn to his stories and his passion for building something he could call his own. At first, I thought my curiosity was simply about supporting and nudging him to get started again. Periodically, I'd ask if he wanted to restart his business. But over time, I realized my attraction to building a business wasn't just for him but for me. I wanted to create something, too.

Gradually, his discontent with his current work situation grew. While the job gave him financial stability, he often expressed frustration that customers didn't seem as satisfied with the service they received. Despite having plenty of money, many felt they weren't getting value for their investment. Julius shared stories of long-standing customers planning to drop maintenance plans because they didn't feel it was worth it anymore. I was beginning to realize that value didn't necessarily mean the cheapest option—it meant quality, trust, and a sense that customers were getting their money's worth. Customers also want to feel like you want their business and that they are important to you.

MY GROWING DISCONTENT

As Julius moved closer to deciding to start his business, I felt edgy and discontent. I missed and longed for daily challenges, problem-solving, helping people, and being creative. Retirement life wasn't enough "soul food." Also, I felt conflicted about splitting my time between Tulsa and Atlanta. I wanted to spend time with both my family and Julius. It was time for him to fish or cut bait...develop a strategy for taking the contractor's exam, turn his dreams into reality, and earn a new title: *Licensed Contractor*. I needed to get on with Deborah's life.

RINGING THE SCHOOL BELL

We reviewed the outline for the HVAC certification exam, and YIKES, a lot had changed over twenty years. Some of the science background information seemed daunting to Julius. When I was in Tulsa, we often used ZOOM at 5 am to review information before Julius had to leave for work. While in Atlanta, I tutored at a GED program for adults, so I was in my element; science, math, and research were my zones. I devised a review course for Julius and made up quizzes to test his knowledge. Consequently, I learned a lot about HVAC fundamentals. I took practice tests for fun. My nerdism was in full swing.

SWIMMING UPSTREAM

I knew nothing about starting a company, so I researched HVAC businesses. My eyes almost popped out of my head when I read, "**First-year failure rate:** Around 70% of new HVAC businesses close within their first year."

As I delved into this new venture, I immersed myself in books, webinars, and live events about launching a business. The more I learned, the more I realized how much I didn't know. My confidence started to shrink, and I questioned whether I could understand what it took to run a business. Moving from a confident newbie to this uncertain stage was a game-changer for me. That's where I opened up—taking in suggestions, advice, criticism, and, most importantly, learning from other people's mistakes and wisdom. Being successful in business isn't just about hard work and working long hours. Based on known statistics, eighty percent of the HVAC businesses that started when we did in 2019 have closed.

> *The best way to succeed in business is by avoiding the mistakes others have made.*

OKIES HEAD BACK HOME

In the fall of 2019, we returned to Tulsa to start the business, naively armed with an LLC certificate; we were ready. We couldn't contain our excitement when we placed the first magnets on our 1996 truck. Our website launched, and I admired our pictures daily. We arranged for our photo shoot to be at the showroom and warehouse of a local distributor. Even before our first customers, we looked like we had a good thing going on.

SURVIVING COVID

In the spring of 2020, business started picking up about the same time the news headlines discussed a mysterious disease called COVID-19. I have worked in medicine for over 30 years. I have seen the ravages of unchecked viral diseases—many of which we couldn't even name, characterize, or control. Because of that experience, I didn't have trouble accepting the precautions. When disposable masks were in short supply, I sewed our cloth masks.

Many HVAC contractors didn't have customers, but we continued to get enough to keep going. Julius adapted to communicate with customers through his mobile phone while looking at them behind locked doors and closed windows. I attended networking groups via Zoom. I learned the basics of social media, which became a lifeline for finding new customers. Together, we adjusted to the "new normal," and despite all the challenges COVID-19 threw our way, we survived 2020!

Gradually, we built our customer base by doing home warranty work. The customers appreciated us for the quality of our work, but the warranty companies were a different story. They seemed more interested in quick, band-aid fixes than real, lasting solutions. This clash in priorities made it clear that home warranty work wasn't the right fit for us, especially when we believed in planning and maintaining equipment to avoid problems in the first place.

FROM MEDICINE TO HVAC: HOW MY MEDICAL BACKGROUND SHAPED MY APPROACH TO CUSTOMER SERVICE

When I first entered the HVAC industry, many business aspects felt daunting—especially pricing structures, inventory management, and marketing. However, one thing that felt natural to me from the very beginning was customer service. That's because, before HVAC, I spent years in medicine.

I learned that every patient wants to feel heard, valued, and understood in medicine. My best medical mentor instilled in me a simple but profound principle: **when you talk to a patient, they should feel like they are the most important person in the world for those moments.** What may be routine to a doctor—a diagnosis, a treatment plan, or a prescription—is often overwhelming and frightening for a patient. They are experiencing something unfamiliar and don't feel in control of their bodies. How we communicate with them can make all the difference in whether they feel reassured or even more anxious.

That lesson carried over into HVAC. A broken air conditioner or heater might be an everyday job for our team. Still, for a homeowner, it can be stressful and even scary—especially when it happens at the worst possible time. They don't just want a solution; they want to feel like their problem matters. They want to know that we see them, that we understand their frustration, and that we are genuinely listening.

Just as a good doctor explains a condition in a way that makes sense to a patient, a good HVAC technician takes the time to explain what's wrong with a system in a way that homeowners can understand. Customer service representatives often give the best explanations because they don't use jargon, just plain basic words. At a job, the technicians are often told that they don't have to explain anything because "Deborah already explained everything to me."

We prioritize showing customers what's happening before talking about solutions. We encourage customers to watch (at a safe distance) while the technicians work. Whether it is showing a broken or burnt-out part or having customers listen to the screeching sound of bearings going out, we want customers to understand the problem. We diagnose, explain, and then prescribe solutions.

Another key lesson from medicine is empathy. A doctor doesn't just treat symptoms; they acknowledge the emotions behind them. In HVAC, we do the same. When a family is sweating through a summer heatwave or shivering in the middle of winter, it's not just about fixing a machine—it's about restoring their comfort, peace of mind, and ability to enjoy their home. We don't rush through appointments or treat customers like just another job on the schedule. Instead, we focus on being present and answering questions.

Ultimately, customer service isn't about selling a product or completing a repair but building trust. Whether in medicine or HVAC, people don't always remember the exact words you said. **Still, they always remember how you made them feel. It's not just what you do but how the customer feels about**

FROM MEDICINE TO ADVENTURE

what you did. My medical background taught me that, and it continues to shape how I serve customers daily.

I can't emphasize enough that customer service is key to staying in business. There will always be another contractor who is cheaper priced. Large companies often buy parts and equipment at discounted prices and offer deeper discounts. Personalized service, feeling they are getting value for their money, and knowing you want them as customers are why customers will choose smaller companies.

LEARNING TOO MUCH TO STAY IN THE BACKGROUND

I was only supposed to help with the business. After the first year, I did it all—scheduling appointments, following up with customers, pricing services, balancing the books, writing ads, managing social media, making videos, writing estimates, and attending networking events. Both Julius and I worked 14-hour days. That which does not kill you makes you strong! I started to view myself not as a support person but, as Julius told others, **"the brains of the business."** I started thinking like a CEO, and it felt good.

DOC J'S HEAT AND AIR: A CUSTOMER SERVICE JOURNEY

When we started Doc J's Heat and Air, we knew customer service had to be more than just a buzzword. We've all heard companies claim they "treat customers like family," but what does that mean? We had to define it for ourselves.

DEFINING EXCEPTIONAL CUSTOMER SERVICE

For us, exceptional service isn't just about fixing HVAC systems; it's about respect and trust. These are some of the tangible ways we define customer service.

- Always wearing shoe covers and cleaning up after ourselves.

- Showing up on time and keeping customers informed if there are delays.

- We introduce ourselves by name and explain our role.

- Listening carefully to customer concerns and answering questions honestly.

- Providing transparent, upfront pricing before any work begins which lessens financial worries.

- Recommending solutions based on what's best for the customer—not just sales targets.

- Giving the customer options so they feel in control of the situation.

- Following up after the job to make sure customers are happy and heard.

MAKING CUSTOMER SERVICE A COMPANY-WIDE STANDARD

One of the hardest lessons we learned early on was that customer service isn't just about the office staff—it has to be part of our culture. No matter how good a technician is at their job, they're not the right fit for our team if they treat a customer poorly.

That's why we:

* ✦ Have a system for daily and weekly feedback to address wins and areas for improvement.

* ✦ Expect every employee, from office staff to technicians, to uphold the same service standards.

* ✦ Reinforce these expectations through training, mentorship, and accountability.

Share and visibly display the notes, letters, and other tokens of appreciation that customers send to our office. These serve as daily reminders of the impact excellent service has.

Our weekly staff feedback system focuses on work habits, technical skills, and customer service. Under the customer service category, we define what excellent service looks like for each position. This helps set clear expectations and ensures that every role contributes to customers' overall experience.

OWNING OUR REPUTATION—NOT LETTING GOOGLE DEFINE IT

Small businesses live and die by their online reputation, but we believe customer feedback should be meaningful—not just a numbers game. Google is a modern-day version of word-of-mouth, helping people learn about our business. But it shouldn't be the only way we share the positive feedback we receive. One of the best ways we communicate what excellent customer service looks like is by sharing what our customers say about us. We proudly showcase the reviews, thank-you cards, and letters we receive. Our technicians have even been gifted brownies, cookies, and fresh eggs from appreciative customers—a testament to the personal relationships we build through excellent service. This personal touch is what makes our service stand out, and our customers feel valued.

WE DON'T PRESSURE OUR TECHNICIANS TO ASK FOR GOOGLE REVIEWS WHILE WORKING. INSTEAD, WE:

- ✦ **Send Out Review Requests Immediately After the Job is done.** This timing is chosen to acknowledge the technicians' hard work and to ensure that customers are most likely to provide thoughtful reviews at this point.

- ✦ **Encourage Direct Feedback** – We address concerns before they escalate, ensuring customers feel heard.

✦ **Share Customer Reviews, Thank-You Notes, and Positive Interactions** – Whether on our website, in our office, or through social media, we celebrate success to recognize the efforts of everyone and to keep the motivation high.

✦ **Focus on Delivering Excellent Service** – We believe great service naturally leads to positive reviews.

✦ **Take the Pressure Off Our Technicians** – We know reviews can reflect factors outside their control, like pricing. While valuable, we don't make Google reviews the primary measure of success. Instead, we rely on internal metrics to evaluate performance and customer satisfaction.

We ask our technicians to treat customers with empathy and respect; we believe they deserve the same in return. They can't provide excellent service unless they feel valued and cared for. That's why we support our team by creating a positive work environment where they can focus on doing their job without the added stress of chasing reviews.

VIEW NEGATIVE FEEDBACK AS A BLESSING, NOT A CURSE

Every positive or negative review is a valuable learning opportunity for us. Positive reviews highlight what we're doing well and reinforce the importance of maintaining high standards. **"When we mess up, we 'fuss up."** So when we get negative reviews, admit our errors, and express a genuine desire to do better in the future. Negative reviews, even those that are unfair give us opportunities to explain the Doc J way of doing business. The first two sentences of our response are meant for the original customer, acknowledging their experience and concerns. The rest is directed to your future customers. We explain our way of doing business and how we provide excellent customer service.

FOLLOWING UP AND CLOSING THE LOOP

One of our most valuable lessons is that a job isn't truly done until we check in with the customer. That's when we get the honest feedback that helps us improve. So, whenever possible, we reach out after service to ask:

- ✦ Was the technician polite and professional?

- ✦ Did they wear shoe covers and introduce themselves?

- ✦ Did they clearly explain the problem and pricing before starting the work?

- ✦ How satisfied are you with the overall service?

Happy customers often leave great reviews; when concerns arise, we can fix them before they become more significant.

I also experienced this in the medical field—following up after procedures made a huge difference in patient satisfaction and care. My dentist still does this, and because of it, I've become one of his most loyal fans. His follow-ups don't just remind me of his excellent service; they make me rave about it to others.

At the end of the day, customer service isn't a department—it's the heart of our business. Our customer-centric approach has helped us build a loyal customer base and improved our service quality and business reputation. We hope other small business owners can take inspiration from our approach and create exceptional service standards, reaping the same benefits as ours.

ABOUT THE AUTHOR

In 2013, Deborah Jenkins retired from her successful medical career, including 12 years with Doctors Without Borders, and returned to her hometown of Tulsa. She looked forward to vacations and family dinners. Unexpectedly, she reconnected through Facebook with her childhood sweetheart and prom date, Julius Warren. He wanted to restart his HVAC business, so Deborah began assisting him with small tasks. Given her driven, curious personality, she dove deep to learn more about heating and air conditioning. She discovered that she had the aptitude to build a thriving business. She wanted a company that gave back to her community, supported employees, and gave opportunities to under-served groups and women. She wanted to build the business in the working-class community where she and Julius grew up.

Because of her healthcare background, Deborah emphasizes listening to clients' needs. Deborah's empathetic approach ensures every customer feels valued, mirroring the care she provides as a physician.

Knowing that women often make vital household decisions but may hesitate to ask questions, Deborah has created a welcoming environment where clients receive clear information about their heating and cooling systems. She initiated "Deborah's Corner," a weekly series offering practical HVAC tips for homeowners.

A vocal advocate for women in the HVAC field, where female technicians comprise less than 2% of the workforce, Deborah is committed to hiring and mentoring women within her company. She aims to empower them to realize their potential and inspire other female entrepreneurs to embrace their "Sparkle Power."

CHAPTER 9

Rooted In Ambition

By Dee Armstrong

Growing up as an only child, I had a front-row seat to entrepreneurship. My parents weren't just business owners— they were dreamers, weaving their ideas into reality. I had the privilege of watching them navigate their journeys, learning from their challenges and successes, and eventually carving out my own path, inspired by their drive and resilience.

My mom's beauty shop was my childhood playground, a space where I learned more than I realized at the time. I wasn't just a kid hanging around—I was a superhero, with her salon apron as my cape. I remember the hum of the blow dryers, the clinking of hair clips, and the smell of perm solution filling the air. Those old-school dryers, with their deep, round hoods, were like spaceships to me. I'd sit beneath them, pretending I was soaring through the stars, blasting off to distant galaxies, completely lost in my imagination. And, of course, I had my cotton-tail experiment stuffing cotton for perms in my pants to make a tail, convinced it was the most brilliant idea ever.

In those small moments, I learned the art of creativity, problem-solving, and business, though I had no idea that's what was happening at the time. I was a sponge, soaking up everything the way my mom interacted with her customers, the rhythm of her work, the way she made people feel valued and seen. She didn't just offer a service; she built relationships. Her warmth and energy were magnetic. I watched her balance everything with grace: her craft, her clients, and the day-to-day challenges of running a business. Every detail of that space, from the buzzing clippers to the laughter of her clients, left a lasting imprint on me.

Being an only child meant I had to get creative to keep myself entertained, and I loved playing store. I'd turn my bedroom into a bustling grocery shop, with imaginary aisles and shelves stocked with make-believe products. I'd pretend to be both cashier and manager, expertly ringing up my own purchases, delighting in the sound of the register clicking and the imaginary "cha-ching!" of a sale. The excitement I felt as I made my transactions felt real—like I was handling actual money, making important decisions. I even convinced my dad to play along, offering him "deals" like "five dollars for a ten," watching his eyes light up with amusement as he went along with my games. He'd laugh, humoring me every time, and that playful interaction felt like a mini business partnership in its own right.

Those early years weren't just about play; they were the foundation of my entrepreneurial spirit. In those small, seemingly insignificant moments, I began to understand the value of creativity, persistence, and human connection. And even as I grew older and ventured out on my own, those lessons stayed with me, guiding my decisions and inspiring the ambitions I continue to pursue.

These weren't just games—they were early lessons in value, negotiation, and connection. I didn't realize it at the time, but every "transaction" I made, every imaginary business I ran, was shaping my understanding of the world in ways I wouldn't fully grasp until later. My parents, grounded in their own experiences, were incredibly open-minded and logical, and they passed those qualities down to me. They didn't just let me dream—they encouraged it, even when my ideas seemed a little out there. My mom, with her unwavering belief in me, would listen to my wild schemes with a smile, never dismissing them, always asking, "How can we make this work?" My dad, too, would lend his thoughtful advice, helping me figure out the practical steps to turn ideas into something real. They taught me that logic and imagination aren't opposites— they're partners, and that's where I found my sweet spot, learning how to blend the two.

Watching my mom run her childcare center was another powerful source of inspiration. She was a force of nature, never missing a day of work in 15 years. Rain or shine, sickness or health, she showed up. Her presence there was a quiet kind of strength—she didn't need to shout or demand attention; she commanded it by being reliable, consistent, and genuinely invested in the kids she cared for. I can still picture the mornings, the smell of breakfast wafting through the air, the sound of little feet running through the hallways, and my mom's voice—calm yet firm—guiding the children. She was their safe place, their steady anchor. It wasn't just about running a business for her; it was about making a difference in the lives of those kids and their families. Her drive was contagious, like a spark that could ignite a fire in anyone who came into contact with it. I remember watching her long hours, the tired but satisfied look on her face when she came home, and feeling a deep sense of respect for her unwavering dedication. She showed me what true passion and grit look like, and it's a lesson that's stayed with me ever since.

My dad, ever the steady partner, balanced her ambition with his grounded perspective. He was the kind of man who measured his words, weighed every option, and thought before acting. He'd sit with me after a tough day, helping me untangle the mess of emotions or problems I was facing, and calmly remind me, "Every problem has a solution. You just need to give it time and think it through." His quiet confidence and patience taught me that challenges weren't something to fear—they were puzzles waiting to be solved. Together, my parents showed me how to dream big while staying firmly rooted in reality. My mom's relentless drive paired with my dad's steady hand created a balance I've carried with me in every step of my journey. They didn't just teach me how to work hard—they taught me how to live with purpose.

> **Takeaway:** Regardless of your industry, customer experience is key. How you make people feel will determine whether they return.

LESSONS FROM THE CLASSROOM

Throughout my school years, I was fortunate to cross paths with a few remarkable teachers who left a lasting imprint on my life. They weren't just educators; they were mentors, guides, and people who saw potential in me that I hadn't yet recognized in myself.

Coach Ham was the first teacher who truly stood out. He taught gym and biology, but his lessons extended far beyond textbooks and drills. He wasn't just about physical strength— he taught us the power of presence. His mantra was simple but profound: **Show up.** Not just with your body, but with intention, with purpose, with your best self. Whether it was a tough workout or a challenging biology exam, he drilled into us that being there, mentally and emotionally, was half the battle. He also encouraged us to stand up for ourselves, a lesson that has served me well in countless situations since. I learned that my voice mattered and that I had the power to claim space, even when I didn't always feel it.

Then there was Coach Carr, who taught me more than just how to parallel park. He taught me how to hold my ground. I can still hear his no-nonsense voice as he looked me in the eye and said, "Don't let anyone push you around." He wasn't just talking about the road; he was talking about life. Coach Carr was the first person who ever taught me to trust my instincts and to never tolerate disrespect—something that's stuck with me in every stage of my life. His lessons weren't about the mechanics of driving; they were about the strength and resilience needed to navigate the road ahead, both on the pavement and in life.

And then there was Mrs. Gardner—*a force of nature* in every sense. She wasn't just a teacher; she was a revolutionary in a classroom full of girls. She made it her mission to show us that there was no dream too big, no ambition too bold. Through her eyes, we learned that women could do absolutely anything—*if* we were willing to fight for it, if we never backed down, no matter how difficult the road. She poured belief into us, especially when we struggled to believe in ourselves. Her fierce dedication to empowering us left an imprint that continues to shape the way I approach challenges today. She taught us to dream fearlessly, to push boundaries, and to never stop until we reached our goals.

> **Takeaway:** Confidence isn't built in grand moments; it's forged in small, everyday choices. It's built when you stand your ground, when you believe in yourself, even if the world is slow to catch up. And most importantly, it's built when you show up—mentally, emotionally, and with purpose.

FROM ACCIDENTAL JOB TO PURPOSEFUL CAREER

I didn't set out to find my career—it found me. What began as a recommendation for a data entry job quickly evolved into something far more meaningful. What I thought was a temporary opportunity turned into a life-changing passion. For seven years, I had the privilege of working under an incredible mentor—the company owner—who shared not only the "how" of business but also the "why." He showed me the ins and outs of what worked, and just as importantly, what didn't. Those lessons were priceless. And when the time came to take a leap, I knew I was ready. I was fueled by the wisdom, support, and tough love I had received along the way.

But let's be honest: every entrepreneur faces setbacks. Failure is a rite of passage. My first stumble? A classic rookie mistake with finances. I'll admit it—things didn't add up, and I quickly realized I had a lot more to learn. But that's where my parents stepped in. They didn't just bail me out—they taught me, showed me how to pick up the pieces, and gave me the perspective I needed to rise from it stronger and more grounded.

The second time? Well, let's just say I missed a critical detail and had to refund a chunk of money I didn't have. It was one of those moments where reality smacks you in the face—and hard. It humbled me in a way that words can't fully capture. But it also opened my eyes. I wasn't just learning about business—I was learning about resilience, accountability, and the courage to face uncomfortable truths. I promised myself that I'd never let that happen again, and to this day, I haven't.

Try This:

The next time you're facing a difficult decision, take a moment to ask yourself:

✴ What's the worst that could happen?

✴ What's the best that could happen?

✴ Can I live with the worst while working toward the best?

BUILDING SOMETHING BIGGER

Life is all about connection. We're all fighting battles, facing struggles, and experiencing triumphs whether or not it's visible on the surface. That's why I make it a priority to lead with empathy and kindness. These aren't just values I hold close; they are the foundation upon which I approach everything— people, work, and life itself. When you approach others with an open heart and a genuine desire to understand, you create an environment where trust, collaboration, and authenticity can flourish.

But connection isn't just about how we interact with others it's also about finding balance within ourselves. I'll be the first to admit that I love the hustle. The grind. There's something energizing about pushing yourself to new limits, achieving more than you thought possible. But I've learned the hard way that without balance, the grind can quickly turn into burnout. You can't do it all on your own, and if you try to, you'll find yourself running on empty before long. That's when I realized the importance of stepping back and recharging. It's not a luxury it's a necessity. And equally important?

Trusting others to help carry the load.

Delegating isn't a sign of weakness; it's a sign of strength. Building trust in my family and my team, both in my personal life and within our companies, has been one of the most critical elements of our success.

Through the work we've done with ECHO Project Management Group, Inc. and Pink Unicorn Ventures, LLC, we've had the privilege of amplifying the voices of over a million people. Crazy, right? But here's the thing: it's never been about the numbers for us. It's about the stories. Every voice represents something deeper a struggle, a triumph, an experience that deserves to be heard. When we amplify someone's voice, we're not just making noise. We're making impact. Every person has something to say, something that matters, and they deserve to be seen, HEARD, and understood. That's what drives us every day—the belief that we are contributing to something far bigger than ourselves.

LEAVING A LEGACY

I used to think success was about never failing. That if you could just avoid mistakes, you'd somehow "make it." But I've learned that true success isn't about never falling—it's about rising every time you do. It's about failing, learning, and most importantly, persevering. Every challenge you face is not a setback—it's the process of building something stronger, something more resilient. So, if you're in the middle of a struggle right now, take a moment and breathe. Trust me— you are growing. Even when it doesn't feel like it, you're laying the foundation for something much bigger than you can see in this moment.

If you take nothing else from my story, let it be this:

- ✦ **Dream big, but stay grounded.** Your wildest ideas can be brought to life, but only if you give them the

DEE ARMSTRONG

structure and discipline they need to thrive. Dreaming without action is just fantasy—dreaming with purpose and commitment is how you change the world.

✦ **Fail fast, but learn faster.** Mistakes are not your enemies—they are your greatest teachers. They are not roadblocks, but stepping stones. Every failure carries a lesson, if you're brave enough to listen and adjust. Embrace them. Let them fuel your growth and keep you moving forward.

✦ **Surround yourself with the right people.** Build a tribe of those who push you to be your best, who challenge you to break through your own limitations, and who cheer for you not just when you win, but when you keep going after you've stumbled. The right people won't just support you—they'll inspire you to be more than you ever imagined.

✦ **Lead with kindness.** We often underestimate the power of a kind word, an act of encouragement, or a moment of genuine care. Never forget that sometimes the smallest acts of kindness can have the biggest ripple effects, changing someone's world in ways you may never fully see. You have the ability to lift others just as much as you lift yourself.

✦ And above all—**don't let fear stop you from taking that first step.** Fear is a natural part of the process, but don't let it paralyze you. Everything you need to succeed is already inside of you—it's there, waiting to be tapped into. You just have to have the courage to trust it and take that first bold step forward. **FEAR**—it has two meanings. You choose: **F**ace **E**verything **A**nd **R**ise, or **F**ear **E**verything **A**nd **R**un.

Your legacy is being written in the moments when you choose to rise, to keep going, to be kind, and to believe in the process. Don't wait for permission. The world is waiting for what you have to offer.

ABOUT THE AUTHOR

Dee Armstrong is a visionary entrepreneur, leader, and creator with a passion for amplifying voices and driving change. As the founder of ECHO Project Management Group, Inc. and Pink Unicorn Ventures, LLC, she has led teams to transform industries and improve lives.

Dee's journey began in her parents' entrepreneurial footsteps, where she discovered a love for creativity and connection. From pretending her mom's salon apron was a superhero cape to crafting imaginary cars with sponges and pie dishes, Dee's childhood was a blend of innovation and boundless imagination. That same creativity has fueled her career, especially her fascination with technology and design, which shaped her approach to solving real-world problems.

Through her companies, Dee and her team have helped over a million people share their stories, ensuring they are HEARD in meaningful ways. She takes pride in building connections, amplifying voices, and creating platforms for change.

Known for her empathy, resilience, and passion, Dee has built a legacy of impact—whether by championing patient voices, volunteering for community causes, or inspiring others to dream big. When she's not spearheading innovative projects and ideas, Dee enjoys painting in nature, learning new things, and spending time listening to and connecting with people, always driven by her belief that every story matters.

CHAPTER 10

The Choice Afghan

By Trish Reed

Have you heard the phrase, "Life is about choices?" Sounds simple, doesn't it? I want this for my family, my kids, my career, my life! POOF! Choice made, life changes!

No, I'm sorry, it doesn't actually work that way. What they don't say is that it's many choices, all put together like a cozy, crocheted afghan with different colors and patterns that wraps you in the warmth of goodness that is your life. But at what point do we know this? When do we figure out that staying in this one location allows you to network with someone who will get you to the next one, who introduces you to a new way of doing things that puts you in a completely different, wonderful direction? Or that removing the toxic person today may affect what happens in five years because you see things differently now and your course has changed? Or something as simple as leaving work early that may have kept you out of harm's way or put you in harm's way based on someone else's choices.

Choices made about 15 years ago started me on the path to becoming a health coach. My thought was to learn how to feel good with my hypothyroidism since doctors didn't seem able to. In my quest to learn more, I found there were many out there like me, searching for a way to feel better. The next choice was to expand my knowledge and become certified so I could help others.

This choice would turn my career in accounting on its ear! I'm going to reinvent myself at 50?

I was certain!

So what happened to me to make that choice?

Somewhere around baby number four, my thyroid decided to check out. I was always active and thin, ran on little sleep, and was healthy. I did my homework and wrote the thesis for my Masters degree between the hours of 11 PM and 4 AM...many nights in a row. That's just who I was. Until I wasn't.

After a few weeks of feeling miserable when my youngest was born, I saw my doctor. He treated me for a flu bug. Then, when I still wasn't better a couple of weeks later, he treated me for something else. A week after that, it was something else. I finally walked into his office and said "Please take my blood and run a test; I'm sick and tired of being sick and tired!" Tests came back: Hypothyroidism. Turns out I became hypothyroid from an unknown cause. Possibly during pregnancy, maybe not; we don't really know. Take this synthetic pill every morning, and you'll feel better.

I took it. I followed directions. I did not feel better.

Years went by. I suffered from migraines, which I'd never had before. The debilitating kind that renders a person useless. I gained weight. My brain was in a fog where I couldn't remember words and just didn't seem like I 'was in there.' My hair was dull and thinning. My skin dry, and my nails brittle.

There didn't seem to be a doctor who was willing to help. "It's all in your head" or, "We can change your meds, but it won't make that much difference" or, "Stay the course, it will correct soon," and my personal favorite, "You're just not used to feeling like this. This is the new normal. You will adjust."

REALLY? I'll adjust?! In a country where almost anything seemed possible, with what was said to be the best medicine in the world, how was I being told, "This is as good as it gets, kid?" I wasn't ready to hear that. I was way too young, and I had a baby! I wasn't going to settle for that.

My choices in life to this point weren't necessarily the best for me. Not the best food, minimal exercise, always running at Mach 10 with fire in my hair, but never having the best interests of my health at the forefront. I didn't realize I didn't have that cozy afghan to curl up in. It became apparent, rather quickly now, that I had to make better choices for my health so I could be a better mom, wife, and human.

I decided to actually study the thyroid and its role in our bodies, as well as things that keep it healthy. I was amazed at the lack of information that was provided by my doctors (plural at this point; I went to many looking for relief). Each piece of knowledge I gained led to more questions and more study— like peeling an onion. That choice to study and do that deep dive was followed by many more choices. Some helped move me forward on my quest, and some took me back to what I knew best. All the while crocheting a cozy afghan for me to curl up with.

Courses that should have taken six months took me a year to complete because, well, life happens, and sometimes a choice is overridden by necessity. But I completed the courses. I learned what the thyroid does and the increased risk of other diseases when not treated properly.

My cozy, comfortable, crocheted afghan was feeling so good!

Was it easy? No. Was it eye-opening and soul-bearing diving deep within myself? Absolutely. Many times, I sat down with myself and asked, "What am I doing? Why not just stick with the accounting profession that I know? Why am I killing myself with impossible schedules when so many other people and things in life need me?"

The answer was that when I made the choice to go this route I knew, deep in my belly, in my soul, in the very fiber of my being, that this is where I needed to be. I was being called to help others, not with their taxes and bookkeeping, but with their health.

While moving through this journey, I encountered a move across country, many job changes, the birth of two grand-children, the graduation from college of a couple of my kids, the return of my son from war, the burial of my mother, my sister, my nephew, and my brother, a horrific accident that almost claimed the life of my husband and the decline of my sister in law's health, placing her in a nursing home with the hope that it was temporary.

Life is hard.
Choices can be hard.
They can be delayed.
They can be expedited.
They can be all yours.

The choice to continue on this quest after all that life happening—some of it because of my choices or, at times, because of the choices of others—was hard sometimes. It required a sit down with myself from time to time and an internal vision board. A decision flowchart to really calculate what the next step should be. When all I really needed to do was take a deep breath and look at my 'why'—what got me on this path to begin with? What pulled me in this direction?

So I grieved, I prayed, I cleaned up, I packed up, I unpacked, I changed my clothes, and I continued to move forward with a happy hitch in my step, not a trudge. Occasionally, the whole 'fake it till you make it' deal, but always with a smile—and the knowledge that things will improve. I had enjoyed the warmth of that cozy afghan before, and I wanted it again!

After all that time, 15 years, I am a certified health coach helping others reclaim their health, helping others learn about what they are battling and what the consequences are if the right choices aren't made. And that, too, is a choice, by the way.

One of my clients was having some major issues, under 40, hypothyroid, gaining weight, and was having trouble at home. She came to me in tears and asked if I could help. We got started right away. We discussed what HER why was...and where she'd like to be and what was a reality, where she was currently and was it a realistic goal. Each week we talked a bit about her menu, (I don't like that word DIET...it's a 4 letter word!) We discussed movement and whether she was getting enough each week. With hard work and tenacity she lost over 50 lbs! I started receiving pictures of her wearing clothes that had been tight and were now hanging very loose and clearly too big for her! It was a wonderful win for her.

Another client was over 70, over stressed and under nourished. She was the care giver of her husband who just didn't seem to be getting better and it was taking a toll on my client. Her 'why' was obvious.

We discussed the importance of her health so she could be there to care of him. We changed the menu, movement was not really an issue as she was very active taking care of every-thing, but she needed flexibility. Her joints were stiff and after a long day of providing care she was in a fair amount of pain.

The food discussion moved to anti-inflammatories, something she could and should eat to help reduce that, and what should be avoided which would cause inflammation. We increased the amount she was eating to get more energy and discussed sleeping habits.

She felt so much better, had an increased range of motion and was sleeping better than she had in years...AND without sleep aides!

Why do I share all this?

Because I know you have a dream. I can see the gleam in your eye! And I know you can, too. Because I want you to know that you are not alone.

Life can be like a speed bump at times, slowing you down, making you take a step away from the ideal path to realize your dreams. Don't let it stop you; slowing down is ok, but don't stop.

Life can be catastrophic as well. Take your break. Do what you need to do to get through whatever is wrong. I'm not minimizing these events; I've had several, and they can make your head spin. You reel from the pain. Whether it is the loss of a loved one, the loss of a job and the benefits that come with it, or any other large event, take your time to heal.

Remember, everyone handles things in their own way. You're creating your afghan in your time, not anyone else's. But you do need to keep your vision and dream in sight. You had a reason to have that dream. You had your 'why;' don't let anything make you lose sight of that.

If you haven't done it yet, make a vision board. Something you can actually look at, not just in your head. It really does help to see that every morning. Someplace on that vision board, write your 'why.' If it's because of your family, add a picture of them. Your vision board should make you smile.

Let's say you want to lose weight and tone your body. You're unhappy with what you see in the mirror, but you're not really sure what to do. You have limited knowledge and can pull too much information from the internet, and much of it is contradictory. How do you start a vision board? Where do you begin?

The first thing you've done is make a choice, a choice to make a change. And that's amazing! You identified that you aren't happy and you want to change. Is your 'why' about losing weight or finding happiness when you look in the mirror? Think about that for a minute. Sit down with yourself and really think about it. Understand that what you see in the mirror will change but that alone does not bring happiness. So, is that really your 'why?' Or is it becoming healthier, mind, body and soul? This part can be frustrating but illuminating. Identifying the reasons behind the 'why' is just as important as identifying the 'why.' Just, please, be honest with yourself.

This is where a good Health Coach comes in. We are trained to help you look within, to identify the 'why' and help bring that to fruition! We will help you distinguish fact from fiction in all that information overload obtained from the internet. We help you be honest with yourself and determine the best course of action to get you where you want to be in the most efficient way possible.

It can be time consuming. That's ok. You're getting to know you. Take the time to put this together.

Am I an expert on this? I like to think I am. Many times I've used vision boards. My 'why' has changed a few times over the years, I've used my Health Coach Techniques on myself and have been coached by fellow coaches. These techniques work.

My 'why' has always been identified and I've had the ability to carve the path needed to get to the finish line.

I have a coach now, in fact. She helps me when the why becomes clouded with life requirements. And with her help, I am able to help others. I am certified to help with your health. Be it physical or mental, health is important. In fact, it's THE most important thing you can have.

Make a choice. Call for help. A coach can be so much help in showing you that you have it in you to do what you need. They can also help you create your own decision flowchart to accomplish what you want to do and help you find that 'why' and make sure it's the *right* 'why.' A coach can help pull thoughts together and perhaps offer a different perspective that will bring clarity for your 'why'...helping to crochet your own cozy afghan.

Did you know that Tiger Woods has a coach? That Michael Jordan had a coach? That Tom Brady had a coach? Every great out there has had a coach, and you should too! Because you are one of the greats, aren't you?

I'm so happy to have been here for you right now. I'd be honored to help you complete your afghan. Please give me a call!

Trish@hotwreck.com 860-HOTWREK (468-9735)

ABOUT THE AUTHOR

Trish decided to change her career path later in life...after suffering with hypothyroidism for so long and longing to be as energetic as she was before. In the quest to find what would work, she came across a health coach class that sounded perfect, so she enrolled and became a certified health coach.

All this new knowledge confirmed what she knew – we are all unique. No wonder the Dr. couldn't get beyond the 'normal test results'!!

With additional research she found yet another amazing class on functional diagnostic nutrition. As a Functional Diagnostic Nutritionist Practioner, Trish knows how we function, what to do to feel better and how to maintain that fabulous feeling that we may have lost so long ago!

If you're looking for more information on Trish or to schedule a call to discuss her services visit www.HotWreck.com. Trish will work with you for a personalized route to health and wellness.

CONCLUSION

Your Next Sparkly Move — Keep the Momentum Going

Look at you, making it all the way to the end of this book. I see you. I know you. You're not just here for inspiration—you're here for action. And you? You're exactly the kind of woman who doesn't just *think* about change. You *make it happen*.

Now let's make sure all this momentum doesn't fizzle out the second you close this book.

LET'S TALK ABOUT YOUR TO-DO LIST (AND WHY IT'S A LIE)

Raise your hand if your to-do list is longer than a CVS receipt. Yep, thought so.

Here's the deal: Most of us are drowning in tasks that keep us *busy* but not *moving forward*. We check off things that don't

163

actually bring us closer to our big, bold dreams, and then wonder why we're exhausted but not making real progress.

IT'S TIME TO STOP MANAGING YOUR TIME AND START MANAGING YOUR ENERGY.

That's why I created my Guide and Planner to Sustainable Self-Care—a powerhouse resource packed with 30+ pages of tools, insights, and strategies to help you stay fueled, focused, and fired up.

One of my favorites? The Overwhelm Assessment & Priority Simplifier—because if decision fatigue has been stealing your sparkle, this is how you steal it back.

- Identify what's really worth your time
- Stop wasting energy on decisions that don't matter
- Get crystal clear on what deserves your focus *right now*

Grab it here: suzannecastle.com/free/self-care

WANT TO EXPERIENCE THE SPARKLE IN PERSON? WELCOME TO VERVE!

Let's be real—some things just hit differently **in the room.**

That's why every year I bring powerhouse women together for **VERVE—The Ultimate Event for Women Ready to Rise.**

VERVE isn't a sit-there-and-take-notes kind of event. It's an immersive, high-energy, action-packed experience designed to pull you out of your rut and drop you into massive momentum.

- **Powerful strategies** to scale your life and business *without burnout*

- **Connections that actually matter** (because your inner circle is everything)

- **That 'Oh hell yes, I'm doing this' moment** you've been waiting for

You've read the book. You've soaked in the wisdom. Now? **It's time to step into the room.**

Grab your spot now: suzannecastle.com/verve

THE SPARKLE EFFECT IS YOURS TO KEEP

Here's the deal: You don't need *one more year* of over-thinking. You don't need one more sign that it's time.

The sign is right here. The time is right now.

Take the next step.

> **Download the tools.**

> > **Show up to VERVE.**

> > > **Make your next move.**

CONCLUSION

Because your brilliance? Your magic? Your next level?

It's not waiting. It's yours for the taking.

And I'll be right here, front row, tossing confetti and cheering you on every step of the way.

All the feels.
Suzanne

www.ingramcontent.com/pod-product-compliance
Lightning Source LLC
Chambersburg PA
CBHW050116210326
41519CB00015BA/3983